# THE LITTLE BOOK OF
# FERRARI

Written by Brian Laban

# THE LITTLE BOOK OF
# FERRARI

This edition first published in the UK in 2005
by Green Umbrella

**www.greenumbrella.co.uk**

© Green Umbrella Publishing 2005

Publishers Jules Gammond, Tim Exell

Printed and bound in China

ISBN 1-905009-18-6

The views in this book are those of the author but they are
general views only and readers are urged to consult the
relevant and qualified specialist for individual advice in
particular situations.

Green Umbrella Sport and Leisure hereby exclude all
liability to the extent permitted by law of any errors or
omissions in this book and for any loss, damage or expense
(whether direct or indirect) suffered by a third party relying
on any information supplied in this book.

All our best endeavours have been made to secure
copyright clearance for every photograph used but in the
event of any copyright owner being overlooked please
address correspondence to Green Umbrella Sport and
Leisure, Old Woking Road, Old Woking, Surrey, GU22 8BF

# Contents

# Chapter 1

# Enzo Ferrari

IT'S MID WINTER, NORTHERN ITALY, February 1898, and it is snowing heavily. Heavily enough, in fact, to prevent one young couple in the area from officially recording the birth of their son until two days after the event, on 20 February after his actual birth on the 18th - so forever after, 20 February 1898 would always be quoted as his birth date. And as it would turn out, that would become typical of the new arrival's relationship with authority and convention almost throughout his life, when he never seemed to have much time for doing things the 'ordinary' way. Because Enzo Anselmo Ferrari, as the boy was officially registered at two days old, would achieve great things, but rarely by working to the book.

The family lived on the outskirts of Modena, where Enzo's father, Alfredo, ran a small but busy metalworking business that, for most of the time, gave the family a fairly comfortable lifestyle. Enzo had an older brother, also called Alfredo, who was two years his senior. They shared many things, including a bedroom when they were young, and a love of homing pigeons, but in one respect they were quite different, and with a surprising twist. Alfredo senior would have liked both boys to follow in his footsteps and become engineers, but while young Alfredo accepted the idea and studied diligently, Enzo (who

opera singer, and in September 1908, he switched ideas again, after his father had taken him to nearby Bologna where he saw Felice Nazzaro's FIAT winning the Coppa Florio road race. Now, the ten-year-old Enzo Ferrari wanted to be a racing driver.

ABOVE Nazzaro in Fiat winning Targa Florio, 1907

CENTRE The 'Prancing Horse' logo made famous by Enzo Ferrari

would become synonymous with some of the most exotic automobile engineering in the world) never showed the remotest interest in formal engineering training, or to be honest in a formal education at all. At school he was far more interested in sports than in academic subjects, and he fulfilled one of his childhood career ambitions by briefly writing local football match reports for the prestigious newspaper Gazzetta dello Sport. But he grew out of an even bigger ambition, to become an

He had already had contact with cars, at a time when they were still rare in rural Italy where the family lived. His father owned one, and had started to service and repair cars for other owners in his workshops. And in his early teens, Enzo himself began to learn how to drive.

At the same time, he was being forced to grow up very quickly. In 1914, World

War I broke out; and in 1916, within months of each other, Enzo's father and brother both died – his father from pneumonia, his brother from an illness contracted during military service. In 1917, Enzo followed him into the army, and was assigned to be a blacksmith, shoeing horses. Like father and older brother, though, he suffered illnesses, and after a round of operations and hospital stays he was discharged in 1918, with what looked like poor prospects for the immediate future.

The family business had died with his father and brother, he had no real qualifications, and there were very few jobs on offer. He found one, though, and with a motoring connection – driving refurbished ex-military light vehicle chassis between Turin and Milan, for a Bolognese engineer who had started a business rebodying them for the civilian market. And it was through this apparently mundane driving job that Enzo Ferrari moved a step closer to that still burning motor sporting ambition.

It happened more through social connections than directly through work, when he would eat and drink in local bars in Milan and happened to meet a number of people who had been involved in motor racing before the war – including Nazzaro, who had stirred his imagination in 1908. More important even than Nazzaro, though, was one Ugo Sivocci, from CMN, another small manufacturer who was converting ex-military vehicles for the civilian market, and who also planned to build more sporting vehicles – which Sivocci was employed to test and race. Very soon, Ferrari had become his test-driving colleague at CMN, and on 5 October 1919, at the Parma Poggio di Bercetta hillclimb, Ferrari became a racing driver, too, taking fourth place in the 3-litre class in a stripped CMN chassis.

A month later, Ferrari and Sivocci both drove for CMN in the gruelling Targa Florio road race in Sicily – supposedly having survived an attack by wolves in the Abruzzi mountains on their way to the start, because Ferrari was carrying a revolver under his seat and his shots attracted a group of local workers who helped drive the wolves away. In the race, Sivocci finished sev-

enth and Ferrari a distant ninth, after more of the dramas that already seemed to go with most of what he did. His fuel tank came loose at the start of the race, and after repairing that at the roadside and driving hard to make up time, he was stopped, very near the end of the race, by a group of policemen protecting the president of Italy, who was making a speech in the nearby village. They wouldn't let Ferrari drive on until the long speech was over, then they would-

n't let him overtake the president's car – so by the time he finished, the official timekeepers had left, and he was only classified as a finisher after pleading to Vincenzino Florio himself, the patron of the race.

He was now taking his racing quite seriously, and in 1920 he went to work, and drive, for the far more famous manufacturer Alfa Romeo. In November he finished second for Alfa in the Targa Florio, and over the next couple of years

ABOVE Enzo Ferrari testing his Alfa-Romeo, 1924

he raced for them many times, and even won on occasion, including 1924 the Circuit of Polesine and the Coppa Acerbo, which was a genuinely important and prestigious event. He was helped by the fact that his more famous team-mate Giuseppe Campari in a newer and faster Alfa broke down early in the race, but Ferrari (and riding mechanic Siena) held off the previously all-conquering Mercedes to win fair and square.

And in between, there was another Ferrari win, in an arguably less important race but with much longer lasting consequences – the origins of the famous prancing horse badge. The 'Cavallino Rampante' (originally on a white background) had been the emblem of flying ace Francesco Baracca, Italy's top-scoring World War I fighter pilot. He had been killed in action on 19 June 1918 over the Austrian front lines, but his emblem had been cut from his wrecked aircraft and returned to his parents as a sign of respect. On 17 June 1923 when Enzo Ferrari won the Circuito del Savio race in Ravenna for Alfa Romeo, Baracca's parents, Count Enrico and Countess Paolina Baracca were watching, and invited Ferrari to visit them at their home – where the Countess dedicated her dead son's prancing horse to the young racing driver from Modena, to bring him luck.

Ferrari, of course, accepted the honour, placed the black horse on a yellow shield representing the civic colour of Modena, crowned it with the Italian tricolor of red, white and green, and used it for the rest of his life.

But that was now taking a

new turn, away from racing and towards team management and, in spite of his early lack of interest, engineering.

First, there were more races, and another hint of Enzo's sometimes hazy true story. In 1923 his friend Sivocci was killed while practicing for the Italian Grand Prix and Ferrari was badly affected. In 1924 he should have driven for Alfa in the Lyons Grand Prix, but he withdrew before the start – officially because he was ill (his health was still a

BELOW Enzo Ferrari driving an Alfa Romeo, 1923

constant problem) but some say because he had a nervous breakdown after Sivocci's death. And although he drove a few more races, and had won perhaps a dozen in all, in January 1932, after the birth of his son Alfredo (soon nicknamed Alfredino, or Dino), Enzo retired for good as a racing driver, to concentrate on his new career - as a racing team manager.

In truth he had been building towards this for some time, and was

**BELOW** Alfa Romeo Bimotore, 1935

proving to be good at it. He was particularly adept (oddly given his lack of training) at recognising engineering talent, and attracting it to Alfa's racing department. So during Ferrari's years of management, Alfa, with engineers like Luigi Bassi and Vittorio Jano, became the make to beat.

With cars like the P1 and P2 and drivers like Campari and Antonio Ascari (also Ferrari's choices), Alfa became regular Grand Prix winners, and in 1925 won the title of World Champions – a

level of success that they held onto for most of the decade, and always with Ferrari in charge.

Right at the end of the 1920s, though, in December 1929, Enzo's path took another twist – officially leaving Alfa and emerging as head of a new Alfa racing team, supported by the company but separated from the car building side. It was called Scuderia Ferrari, and in place of the green four-leaf-clover 'Quadrifoglio' badge, it now carried the Prancing Horse.

ABOVE Alfa Romeo P3, 1935

ABOVE Official team drivers, Varzi and Chiron driving an Alfa Romeo P3, 1934

legendary Tazio Nuvolari. Between them, and with the genius of Jano in particular creating ever greater cars, they won everything from the Targa Florio to the Mille Miglia road races, and from numerous Grands Prix to the Le Mans 24-Hour race. Even when Alfa was taken over by the government, the race team was still run by Ferrari, and continued to win through the 1930s until the cars from Italy were finally overwhelmed after 1937 by the Nazi government-backed Mercedes-Benz and Auto-Union Grand Prix 'Silver Arrows'.

Enzo, and Scuderia Ferrari, though, had already built a reputation second to none, and now he planned to take on the Germans with a car of his own, designed by another engineering genius, Gioacchino Colombo. It never raced under Ferrari's name, but as Enzo himself described it, it was taken over

Ferrari moved the team from Milan to Modena and ran Alfas for both official team drivers and for several private owners. And Ferrari continued to attract the best, including Campari, Louis Chiron, Achille Varzi, and arguably the greatest of them all, the by Alfa as they returned to racing in their own right, and Ferrari was invited to manage the new Alfa Corse team which ran it in a handful of races, just below Grand Prix level, before World War II began.

Even before that happened, Ferrari had fallen out with Alfa, after major personality clashes with some of the other people involved in the team, and in effect that was the final move in the early part of the game that was building up to Ferrari becoming a car maker in his own right.

BELOW Auto Union Silver Arrows Grand Prix team

# Chapter 2

# Twist in the Tale

NATURALLY, THOUGH, given Ferrari's character and past history, it was never as simple as that - and now came the next, brief twist in the tale.

Ferrari left Alfa in 1939 with a reasonable financial settlement but a restriction on racing against them under his own name for a period of four years. Which was why, immediately after leaving Alfa, he created a new company called Auto Avio Costruzione – an engineering and design agency, with staff including the brilliant Bazzi, to build sporting cars that would be Ferraris in everything but name. And he started even as the war

was starting, entering two Auto Avio Costruzione 815 sports cars in a race that (thanks largely to the Germans) was actually held after the war had started but before it called a complete halt – the Brescia Grand Prix, which was nominally a version of the Mille Miglia, ran in April 1940.

The 815s had in-line eight-cylinder 1.5-litre engines, based on four-cylinder

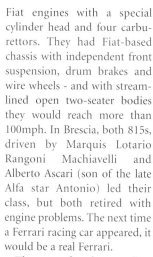

Fiat engines with a special cylinder head and four carburettors. They had Fiat-based chassis with independent front suspension, drum brakes and wire wheels - and with streamlined open two-seater bodies they would reach more than 100mph. In Brescia, both 815s, driven by Marquis Lotario Rangoni Machiavelli and Alberto Ascari (son of the late Alfa star Antonio) led their class, but both retired with engine problems. The next time a Ferrari racing car appeared, it would be a real Ferrari.

That was after the war, during which Alfa's four-year restriction on Ferrari racing under his own name had conveniently expired. And Ferrari had also done well with Auto Avio Costruzione, which he had moved from Modena to nearby Maranello in 1943, where it had grown quite large (in spite of being bombed more than once) while working for the military. Now, in spite of Italy being badly hurt by the war, in spite of the lack of materials and the lack of money, Ferrari planned to make exotic (and by extension expensive) cars – and to start making them as soon as possible.

He also meant to go racing again as soon as there was racing to go to, and in a philosophy that he would stick to for virtually his whole life, he planned to pay for the team's racing by selling cars to customers.

So his first plans after the war, when the company was still called Auto Avio Costruzione, were to build a range of Ferrari sports cars, sports racing cars, and even Grand Prix cars, because whatever else Ferrari may have been short of in 1945, he had ambition in abundance.

In 1946 he announced his plans, and in March 1947 he showed the first car finally to bear his own name – the Ferrari 125. It was an open two-seater sports car, and its superb 1.5-litre V12 engine was designed by Colombo, who (after designing Alfa's first postwar Grand Prix car, the all-conquering 158 Alfetta) had returned to join Ferrari and the faithful Bazzi. The 125cc capacity of

ABOVE Ferrari and Alberto Ascari before the Italian Grand Prix, 1950

OPPOSITE Juan Manuel Fangio in a Ferrari in Italy, 1949

ABOVE 125, 1951

one of its tiny cylinders gave the car its type number, starting a Ferrari tradition. And Ferrari intended to build a series of them for different roles, from roadgoing customer sports car to full-blown racing car. But in the end he built only two examples – one Sport, with streamlined body by Touring of Milan, the other the Competizione, with cycle-type wings that could be left on for sports car races or taken off for Grand Prix type races, even though it was still a two-seater.

Then in May 1947, the 125, the first car ever to be badged Ferrari, appeared in its first race, a small sports car race at Piacenza in northern Italy. Of the two entered (the only two that existed in fact), Giuseppe Farina's crashed in practice and didn't make it to the race, while Franco Cortese's led until two laps from the end when its fuel pump broke. But it was only two weeks until Cortese won the first ever victory for the new marque, in another fairly minor sports car race, in Rome – and before the end of the year, Cortese, Nuvolari and Raymond Sommer had given Ferrari several more wins, making sure the new cars were getting noticed.

And in another move that would continue to be Ferrari practice from here on, even before the first cars started winning, Enzo and his small team were already well advanced with the design of the next evolution, which in the case of the 125 appeared before 1947 was over, in the form of the 159 – whose type number revealed a 1.9-litre development of the original 1.5 V12 engine, with few other changes from the original 125s.

BELOW Giuseppe Farina in his Alfa Romeo Tipo 158, 1950

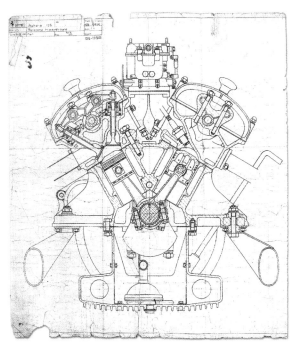

prompted by the introduction of a new Formula 2 racing category in 1947, but it was as short-lived as the first 125 and only two more cars were built before the next version, the 166, followed – this time with a full 2-litre capacity to capitalise on that new Formula 2, as well as to double up as a hugely effective racing sports car.

The 166 was the car that took Ferrari to the next level, both in competition and (on the strength of its racing successes) commercially. In 1948, Clemente Biondetti won the Mille Miglia with an open-topped 166 Sport, and the Targa Florio with a 166 coupe – and won both races for Ferrari again in 1949. Their reputation was growing fast. But that early success was nothing alongside Ferrari's most remarkable triumph of 1948, when the new marque won the greatest sports car race of them all, the Le Mans 24 Hours, at its first attempt, in the first running of the endurance classic after World War II had called a halt. At Le Mans, one of the two 166 Barchettas (an open body style, literally meaning 'little boat') ran near the front in the early hours but crashed before darkness fell. The other, driven by Luigi Chinetti and Lord Selsdon, took the

He had created the 125 with its original engine size because that 1.5-litre capacity, with supercharging, would have been eligible for the Grand Prix formula of the time (which also allowed non-supercharged 4.5-litre engines), had Ferrari had the resources to make the changes. The bigger 159 engine was lead during the night and hung on to win by just one lap, driven mainly by Chinetti, as Selsdon fell ill.

In one swoop, Ferrari had become one of the best known sports car names in the world – including America, where winning driver Chinetti had emigrated from his native Italy, and was about to become Ferrari's first dealer. The first car he imported was a 166 Spyder Corsa, the sports racing version, which was sold to American sports car fan (and all-round sporting hero) Briggs Cunningham – who promptly used it to score Ferrari's first ever racing victory in the USA, at Watkins Glen, New York, in 1949.

With events like these, Ferrari was clearly moving on very quickly indeed, and in fact by 1948 the new marque even kicked off what would become an extraordinary Grand Prix career. That was as planned, with a supercharged and stripped bare version of the 1.5-litre 125, whose superb overhead camshaft

BELOW 166 Barchetta, 1950

engine was one of the most technically advanced in the world when it was introduced, and grew even more sophisticated as it was developed through racing. After running stripped two-seater 125s in lesser races, the first genuine single-seater Formula 1 version, the 125 GP, was introduced in September 1948, with a tubular frame, all independent suspension (where the two-seaters had non-independent rear axles), a five-

speed gearbox in unit with the engine, and about 230bhp from the first supercharged version of the 1.5 V12.

Its first race was the Italian Grand Prix in Turin, and Ferrari entered three cars, for Sommer, Farina and the wealthy and talented amateur racer, Prince Bira of Siam. Farina crashed and Bira suffered Ferrari's regular early problem with a broken gearbox, but from the front row of the grid, in a wet race, Sommer finished third behind an Alfa and a Maserati - Italy's other major sports and racing car manufacturers, both of which had been around for rather longer than newcomer Ferrari. Then on only the 125 GP's second appearance, Sommer scored its first win, in a race at Lake Garda, but there were no more victories that year.

During 1949 the 125 GPs took wins in the Swiss and Czech Grands Prix, in the European Grand Prix at Monza, and in the Dutch Grand Prix – plus the important Daily Express Trophy Race at Silverstone. Meanwhile, the sports cars were racking up big results, too, as their development continued with the 2.3-litre 195 and 2.5-litre 212 versions. Chinetti won the Spa 24 Hour race with the classic 166 in 1949; Gianni Marzotto won the 1950 Mille Miglia with a 195S Berlinetta; and in 1951 Chinetti and Piero Taruffi won the world's most gruelling road race, the mountainous but super-fast 2000-

mile Carrera Panamericana on the US/Mexican borders, with a 212. Sommer had also given Ferrari their first Formula 2 win, in Florence in 1947, with the car designed for exactly that purpose, the 166 prototype – still in effect a stripped sports car, and still a two-seater with the passenger seat removed and the space covered over.

But as with Formula 1, it wasn't long before Ferrari created a true Formula 2 single-seater, the 166 F2, which was also available (at a price) to private entrants. It won all five races that Ferrari entered in the 1949 Formula 2 championship, including taking the top five places in the Bari Grand Prix. In 1950 and 1951 they again won every race they entered, before leaving Formula 2 to concentrate on Formula 1 – while private customers continued in Formula 2, and continued winning.

# Ferrari Style

NOT SURPRISINGLY ALL OF THIS attention was making Ferrari a well known name, and bringing potential customers to Maranello's door. And with the 166, Ferrari had a car with which he could finally do what he'd always intended, to sell both customer racing cars and genuine road cars to finance the 'works' racing programme, and the company's growth. So alongside the racing 166s there first appeared the 166 Sport (a milder, 90bhp version, of which just one spyder and one coupe were built) and then, from the end of 1948, a series of spyders and coupes, the 166 MM sports racer (named for the 166's Mille Miglia win) and the 166 Inter roadgoing sports car – which, together, over the next three

ABOVE 166 Barchetta interior, 1949

years sold in respectable numbers, turning Ferrari into a real manufacturer.

They introduced another Ferrari theme – a variety of styles and different coachbuilders, clothing bare chassis supplied by the Ferrari factory. In the case of the 166 that meant a tubular frame, five-speed gearbox, independent front and live-axle rear suspension, drum brakes, and between 110bhp for an Inter (for a top speed of around

different body styles and different states of engine tune depending on whether the car was to be used purely as a road car, for mixed road and race use, or as a racer. The road cars in particular were growing more user-friendly, too, with ongoing mechanical improvements to both chassis and engines, but also with progressively better trim, and more comfort equipment. By 1952, with triple carburettors and new cylinder heads, the 212 Inter had 170bhp and a top speed of more than 125mph, which made it one of the fastest production cars in the world in its day, spreading Ferrari's fame even wider, and rapidly increasing demand for the customer cars.

It also started one of Ferrari's greatest partnerships, when coachbuilder Pinin Farina (later to become Pininfarina) created their first Ferrari body for a 212 Inter, in 1952. Within a year they were putting more bodies on Ferraris than all other coachbuilders combined. And in two years from 1951 to 1952 Ferrari would build more than a hundred 212's for road and track – but that was still only the beginning. Now, America was calling.

America, however, didn't necessarily want the same kind of Ferrari that worked for Europe, or even the same

105mph) and 150 for the more race-bred MM (which would do almost 140mph).

And all of this set the scene for Ferrari's rapid growth as a car builder into the 1950s, and for even more spectacular racing successes. The production cars, meanwhile, naturally followed the progression of the race cars, with 195 and 212 models following the 125, 159 and 166 lines, and Ferrari offering more variations for each model, with kind of Ferrari that had won the Le Mans 24-Hour race in 1948 (and in doing so created that first awareness of the new name on the other side of the Atlantic). Because basically, America didn't really understand small engines, even if they were as sophisticated as Ferrari's Colombo-designed V12s. What America knew best was cubic inches, and lots of them, so Ferrari gave them a new, and larger alternative.

It came from a different designer, Aurelio Lampredi, as Colombo had left Ferrari in 1950 after falling out with Enzo. So while developments of Colombo's small V12s would take care of Europe for some time to come, Lampredi's much bigger new engines were just the thing for America.

Designed originally for sports car racing, and for Grand Prix racing in large unsupercharged form, Lampredi's first V12 was far bigger than the super-compact Colombo engines, with scope for much larger capacity. In fact it started at 3.3 litres, more than twice the

BELOW 212, 1951

capacity of the first Colombo engines and already bigger than that engine could reasonably stretch to. It had many other differences, too, from cylinder heads and valve operation to the way it was built. It debuted in the 1950 Mille Miglia in the 275S and was fitted into a development of the 125 chassis for the Belgian Grand Prix in June, as the 275 F1. Within a couple of months it had reached the full 4.5 litres allowed by Formula 1 for unsupercharged cars, and had become the 375 F1 – which would be Ferrari's weapon of choice when the new official World Championships for Drivers and for Formula One Manufacturers were launched, for the 1950 season.

BELOW 375 MM, 1953

But away from the race track, Lampredi's engine was about to hit America in a very different kind of Ferrari, introduced at the Paris Motor Show in October 1950 as the 340 America. Not only did it have the bigger, more powerful V12 (4.1 litres and 220bhp as a road car), it had a bigger, stronger chassis and a typically wide range of body styles from several coachbuilders including Vignale, Ghia and Touring – and it was good for more than 140mph. Racing versions were more powerful and faster still, and the 340 Mexico and 340 MM versions respectively finished third in the 1952 Carrera Panamericana and won the 1952 Mille Miglia.

On both road and track it followed the same path as the Colombo-engined cars, and grew in both power and refinement. In 1952 the short-lived 342 America suggested the market didn't want a more comfortable and better equipped Ferrari if it was also less powerful and heavier. So in 1953 Ferrari unveiled the 375 America, with 4.5 litres, 300bhp and the most performance of any 'production' Ferrari so far. But there was still more to come, and only a dozen or so 375s had been built before Ferrari introduced an even more dramatic Lampredi V12-powered car, the 410 Superamerica in 1956 – but that's getting ahead of the story.

# Chapter 4

# The 50s

BACK IN EUROPE IN THE EARLY 1950s, the smaller V12-powered models remained the core of the business, but with the next capacity increase for the still brilliant Colombo V12, Ferrari reached both a type number and a model family that would outlive all the others and serve the marque well for more than a decade. The ground break-ing 250 had arrived.

The number meant a capacity of 3 litres, exactly double that of the origi-nal Colombo V12 that it had grown out of, and (limited by the bore size) about as far as it could stretch with the original block dimensions. But cru-cially, it was very little heavier than the first 1.5, and very much lighter than the big V12 family. It was good for just about everything, It was a perfect capacity for sports car racing, which was Ferrari's next priority after Grand

LEFT 250 MM, 1953

Prix and had a very high profile in the early 1950s. Equally important, it guaranteed lots of customers with racing plans. And finally, it promised superb road cars. All of which, as well as delivering literally hundreds of motor sport victories (including a second Le Mans win against some of the toughest opposition ever) would bring almost two and a half thousand sales over the years and change Ferrari once and for all.

Until now, Ferrari had sold cars only in whatever numbers he needed to support his racing. In fact in its first four years, Ferrari had built fewer than a hundred cars in total. Which was both a wasted opportunity and left Ferrari with very little, if any, profit - in spite of the company now being quite a large, high maintenance organisation.

And of course, the change started with another racing car, the one-off Vignale-bodied 250S sports car that was produced in 1952 - and which, thanks to a sensational drive by Giovanni Bracco, won that year's Mille Miglia, beating the might of the Mercedes-Benz works team and their legendary 'gullwing' 300SL racers. Which led directly to the 250 MM (for Mille Miglia) production

car being introduced at the Paris Show in October.

In that form, it gave 240bhp and around 155mph, which was right at the top of the performance tree in 1952; and as ever there was a choice of shapes – notably Pinin Farina Berlinettas (literally 'little saloons', though we'd probably call them coupes) and open Vignale Spyders.

Oddly, the next 250, the 250 Europa, introduced in Paris in 1953, wasn't a 'real' 250 at all, but a smaller-engined version of the 375 America and a bit of a dead-end experiment in downsizing the Lampredi V12 range. Ferrari knew immediately, however, that the 'Colombo' 250 could be a winner commercially as well as on the race track, and the 1954 Paris Show brought the 'second series' 250 Europa - the true successor to the 250 MM. It came to be known properly as the 250 GT Europa, and this one was a real classic. It was also the first car that Ferrari designed as a more or less standard model. All but one of the 36 built were bodied by Pinin Farina, and while there were detail differences they were all very similar coupes, and very handsome behind their 'egg-crate' grilles.

It was more powerful than the Lampredi Europa, more compact, and lighter – and though not quite as quick as the race-bred MM it was more civilised, more comfortable and better equipped as a road car; a real Grand Tourer in fact, that in true Ferrari fashion could double as a racer.

But road car developments apart, Enzo made absolutely sure that racing still dominated the company – and here as in the production market, the small and large V12 families, plus four- and six-cylinder racing models, lived side by side, to suit every racing need from Grands Prix to Le Mans.

It was what still drove him more than anything else, and in July 1951, Ferrari marked an emotional milestone at the British Grand Prix at Silverstone. It was the second year of the new World Championship and Ferrari's second serious season in Grand Prix racing; and he had switched from the supercharged 1.5-litre 125s to the unsupercharged 4.5-litre 375 F1 which had debuted at the Italian Grand Prix in September 1950. But Ferrari had yet to win a championship race against the all-conquering Alfa 158/159 Alfettas. At Silverstone, Ferrari finally beat Alfa

OPPOSITE 250 Europa, 1953

VANDERVELL LEAD INDIUM BEARINGS

Thin Wall Special

enthusiasm were tears of pain. Because on that day I thought, "I have killed my mother"...'

But now that Ferrari knew how to win Grands Prix, the floodgates opened. They won two more that year, in Germany and Italy, but Alfa took the title. Then in 1952, Alberto Ascari gave Ferrari their first Grand Prix World Championship – and it hardly matters that Alfa had retired and the organisers had ruled that for the next two years the title would be fought by Formula 2, not Formula 1 cars. Ferrari already had clearly the best of those, in the 2-litre four-cylinder 500 F2, and in 1952 Ascari won five Grands Prix and Taruffi the other. Then in 1953 Ascari won five more, Mike Hawthorn won one and Farina one – all with the unbeatable 500 F2.

He wasn't quite so successful in the very different arena of Indianapolis, where the two-and-a-half-mile banked oval and 500 miles of flat-out racing were still dominated by the highly specialised American 'roadsters', almost all powered by the remarkable four-cylinder Offenhauser engine running on

head to head, as Argentine star Froilan Gonzalez won fair and square, with the 375 F1.

Over the next five decades, Ferrari would go on to win more Grands Prix victories than any other manufacturer (as of the middle of 2005, fourteen Formula 1 Manufacturers' titles, and fast approaching 200 Grands Prix wins), but to Enzo Ferrari himself, that day in 1951, beating the current world champions and the team he had grown up with for some 20 years, was perhaps the most emotional victory of all. As he said himself, 'I cried for joy. But my tears of exotic alcohol fuels. Chinetti persuaded Ferrari to give it a try, though, and he did, in 1952, when the Indy 500 was officially a round of the Grand Prix World Championship even though its technical regulations were nothing like Formula 1! They were close enough, though, for Ferrari to adopt four of the 4.5-litre 375 F1 V12s to become 375 Indianapolis cars. Three private entries (run by the Grant Piston Ring team) failed to qualify; Ascari in the official Ferrari entry got as high as sixth before the car succumbed to Indianapolis's extreme stresses, and although there were thoughts of a return over the next couple of years, Ferrari never did go back, and no one else ever ran a Ferrari

BELOW 500 F2, 1959

just twice, and Ferrari contested the second one, in 1958, with three cars against the other European challengers and a good turnout of Indianapolis stars, who were even faster on the high-banked Italian track than on the gently-banked Indy oval. Ferrari entered three cars, one of them developed from the old 375 Indianapolis car from 1952, one 412 MI

ABOVE Dino V6 engine

at the famous 'Brickyard' – making the Indianapolis 500 the only race in the world of any stature that Ferrari has never won.

There was a postscript to the Indy effort, too, some years later at Monza, where a unique event, The Race of Two Worlds, brought the Indy drivers and the Europeans together on the high-banked Monza autodrome for what would be the fastest race in the world – Indianapolis included. The event ran

'Monza Indianapolis' single-seater created from the recent Formula 1 racer, and the 296 MI, a 3-litre version of the current 246 F1 Dino. The old 375 (driven by American Harry Schell) broke in the second heat; the 412 MI took pole position at almost 175mph and led, but with major tyre wear problems finished only third; and the 296 MI

simply wasn't fast enough.

So far as the rest of the 1950s went, that was one of Ferrari's few low points, although 1954 had been another one. The World Championship was for a new Formula 1, for unsupercharged 2.5-litre cars, and although Ferrari had two promising four-cylinder cars (both evolved from Formula 2 models) in their 625 F1 and 553 F1 'Squalo', plus drivers of the quality of Hawthorn, Farina and Gonzalez, they

ABOVE AND LEFT
246 GP, 1959

Fangio in his D50 Lancia-Ferrari at the 1956 French Grand Prix

of six and only Maurice Trintignant put Ferrari in the winner's circle, with the ageing 625 in the Monaco Grand Prix.

In 1956 they bounced back, with V8-powered cars inherited from the Lancia team - disbanded as the company was in financial trouble, and after their star driver, Ascari, had been killed (ironically, testing a Ferrari sports car at Monza in 1955). They ran as Lancia-Ferraris in 1956 and 1957, with Juan-Manuel Fangio giving Ferrari their third title in his first season with the team, partnered by British star Peter Collins. But in 1957 it all unravelled again, the cars were outclassed, and were generally outpaced by both Maserati and the returning Mercedes-Benz, and only won two Grands Prix that year. And they were well beaten again in 1955 as Mercedes won five out Fangio took the title away to new employers Maserati, with Ferrari failing to win a race.

Again, it was a temporary lull, as 1958 saw the return of a pure Ferrari

Formula 1 car in the V6-engined Dino 246 F1, and ended with Hawthorn being crowned as the first ever British champion, even though he'd only won one Grand Prix, in France. Stirling Moss had won four (with Cooper and Vanwall) but Hawthorn was never out of the podium finishers and won through consistency. Sadly, his Ferrari team-mate and best friend, Collins, who had won the British Grand Prix, was killed at the Nurburgring, and Hawthorn, having already announced his retirement, died in a road accident

BELOW Mike Hawthorn in his Ferrari during practice for the British Grand Prix, 1958

in January 1959, tingeing the triumph with sadness.

The Dino story contained sadness of a different sort, too, especially for Enzo Ferrari himself. The Dino name that first appeared on the front-engined 246 F1 paid tribute to the son who died, Enzo's only legitimate son from his marriage to Laura in the early 1920s. He was born on 19 January 1932, leading his father to give up his racing career. He was christened Alfredo, like the grandfather and uncle who'd died long before he was born; his nickname was Alfredino, or 'little Alfredo', which became Dino.

Enzo was devoted to him and once the Ferrari company was created he did everything to involve him in its running – and unlike his father, Dino had some real engineering training, as well as studying economics. But like his father, as a young man he was frequently ill, with what turned out to be muscular dystrophy. The eventual outcome was inevitable, but even as he grew weaker, Dino spent much of his time around the factory, and his father credited him with the concept, if not the detail, of the V6 engine for the late 1950s Formula 2 cars – a layout later adapted for the 1.5-litre Formula 1 regulations, as well as for sports car racing, for hillclimbing, for road cars and even (in the Lancia Stratos) for world championship rallying.

The first Dino V6 ran just before Dino died, on 30 June 1956, aged just 24. His father mourned him to the end of his own life, visiting his grave every single day, and leaving Dino's office in the Maranello factory exactly as his son had left it the last time he was there. Except that where Dino

ABOVE Enzo Ferrari behind the wheel of one of his cars

had sat, there was now just a photograph. What might have happened in the company had Dino lived and eventually taken over from his father we'll never know. But Enzo's personal loss was total.

# Chapter 5

# Pinin Farina

WHATEVER, WHILE ALL THESE events were unfolding on the race track and in Enzo Ferrari's private life, the production side of the company was going from strength to strength, as both V12 families evolved and prospered in their own directions. In America, the 410 Superamerica, as launched in January 1956 with 5-litre V12 and at least 340bhp, evolved through two more variations which included a shorter wheelbase at the end of 1956 and more power (around 360bhp) in 1957. Pinin Farina bodied most of them, but as in the old days in Europe, almost no two were exactly alike – although the Superamerica's price meant that hardly mattered. And before the big and luxurious but stunningly quick coupe reached the end of its production life in 1959, it had formed the basis for its own successor

– although that wouldn't appear in production until 1964.

On the other side of the Atlantic (not that the smaller V12s weren't exported, too), the 250 family was also growing up in its own way. Not getting bigger engines, obviously, but continuosly getting more power, more performance, more sophisticated chassis, and more customers.

While Pinin Farina built much bigger new premises, between 1955 and 1958, some coach-building was farmed out to Carrozzeria Boano, who built around 130 GTs – the early ones known as 'Boanos', after Mario Boano who founded the company, the later ones 'Ellenas', after he moved to Fiat and his son-in-law Ezio Ellena took over until Pinin Farina returned.

The styling didn't change much, but with their new, larger premises, production numbers did – growing dramatically. And now Ferrari (prompted by Pinin Farina who were always looking for new ideas) was about to take it to another level again, by creating a Ferrari to appeal to a whole new segment of the market – the 250 GT Cabriolet, introduced in 1957.

There had been open Ferraris before, of course, even one-off cabriolets, and Pinin Farina had recently built several open concept cars, but this was really Ferrari's first series-production convertible, and it combined performance with style, luxury, long distance comfort, and a very up-market, fully-trimmed, fully-weatherproof folding roof. The first series, from 1957 to 1959, was beautiful; the next was even more so, as Cabriolet styling was updated alongside the coupes. And the Cabriolets got more power, too, as the 3-litre V12 was improved again. It even got disc brakes, which Ferrari had

**LEFT** Battista Pinin Farina, 1960

**BELOW** 250 Cabriolet Pininfarina

resisted for too long, and it was widely admired as a real luxury tourer with huge performance, from around 240bhp. All of which added up to Ferrari's biggest sellers so far – which made it slightly strange that when production ended in 1962, Ferrari wouldn't offer a direct cabriolet replacement for almost exactly two years.

For America, in the 250 family, there was a different kind of soft-top, if anything even more stunning than the European Cabriolet. This was the 250 GT California Spyder, and where the Cabrio was strictly a tourer, the Spyder was light, simple and powerful enough to double occasionally as a weekend race car. It was styled, again, by Pinin Farina, and looked subtly more muscular and sporty. It was based on a more competition-oriented 250 GT, the Tour de France Berlinetta that was one of Ferrari's classic road/race crossover designs. And the California would still be quite civilised, but it would be more simply equipped than the Cabriolet, lighter, more agile and faster. It started with 250bhp, but you could have more power and less weight with special aluminium body panels. Then the second generation moved the goalposts again, with 280bhp or more, a shorter wheelbase, better suspension, brakes and transmission, and a top speed of 145mph or more. It also looked absolutely stunning, and it stayed in production until 1963, selling in very respectable numbers.

The car it had been based on, the Tour de France (and its close relatives) showed, however, that while Ferrari was catering for a more sybaritic customer in one direction, he wasn't losing sight of the all important racing connections in the other direction. It was officially called the 250 GT Berlinetta, Ferrari's name for the lighter, more stripped out, more dual-purpose coupe, in this case introduced in 1956 – and taking its unofficial name from Alfonso de Portago's win in the Tour de France Automobile that year with an earlier version of the 250 GT.

BELOW 250 Tour de France

But from 1959 its 'dual-purpose' successor was even more successful – the classic 250 GT SWB, short wheelbase. It reflected Ferrari's new focus on GT racing now that category became the premier sports racing class after the 1955 Le Mans disaster, when more than eighty spectators died after Pierre Levegh's Mercedes 'prototype' sports car racer crashed into crowded spectator terraces. It evolved from the Tour de France and it was sold in both road and racing versions, although either could at a pinch be used for the other role.

It was massively successful. Road versions had 240bhp, the final, most extreme racers had up to 300bhp. It had a very stiff chassis, improved suspension, and disc brakes. Styled by Pininfarina (as they'd now become) it showed how aerodynamics were becoming more important. It also said something about racing rules that required a certain number to be built to qualify for the GT class. Which meant Ferrari had to sell customer cars, and some of those more aimed at occasional (even non-) racers – those SWBs with mainly steel bodies where the full competition ones were mainly aluminium, glass where they had plastic windows, and some interior trim where the real racers had none. Even the road car, however, would beat 155mph, and any 250 GT SWB was a serious supercar.

It followed a fine period for Ferrari's sports car racers, the V12, V8 six- and four-cylinder models that through the 1950s had won every sports car race of any consequence at least once. And that included the Mille Miglia, the Targa Florio, the Carrera Panamericana, the Spa 24 Hours, the 12 Hours of Sebring, and the biggest of them all, the Le Mans 24 Hours. The second win there came in 1954, when Ferrari retained the sports car championship they had won in 1953, in the first year of the official title. Between 1953 and 1961 they would only lose the sports car title twice, to Mercedes. And the sports racing cars of this golden age included the 290, the 315 and 335, the 500 Mondial and Testa Rossa, the 625 Targa Florio and Le Mans models,

and the 750 and 860 Monzas. Then there were the six-cylinder gems, the 376S and 446S, not to mention the catalogue of great GT cars, and the legendary 250 Testa Rossa (named for the red crackle paint colour of its camshaft covers) which was possibly the most famous sports racing Ferrari of them all in those glorious years.

Introduced in 1957, it was affected by rule changes after the Le Mans disaster, but it was still a prolific winner, giving

BELOW Castelloti followed by Hawthorn and Fangio at Le Mans 1955

Ferrari a third Le Mans win in 1958, with Phil Hill and Olivier Gendebien – before a run of Ferrari Le Mans victories in every year from 1960 to 1965, with cars such as the 250 Testa Rossa, the 330P (that was P for Prototype), 250P and the beautiful 250LM. And that was a Le Mans record that remained unbeaten until Ferrari pulled out of sports car racing (Enzo argued continuously with the rule makers) and Porsche took up their multiple-race-winning mantle.

On the road, the 250 family continued to evolve in whatever direction Ferrari saw a potential market. With the 250 GT 2+2 (or 250 GTE) between 1960 and 1963, he introduced his first real four-seater (as opposed to two-seaters with two token spaces) – and almost a family Ferrari! It was introduced at Le Mans in 1960, not in the race, but as the pace car, and it went into production in October, with 240bhp and a top speed of about 135mph, but with genuine long distance comfort and practicality for two adults and two children. Strange though it may have seemed to Ferrari at the time, it became a big seller, with around 950 built; and alongside it, Ferrari created another 250 variant that showed he was increasingly happy to supply customers with no interest in racing.

This one was the 250 GT Berlinetta Lusso, and not only was it one of the most beautiful cars in the 250 range, it was one of the most significant. The Lusso name (meaning luxurious) was showing that Ferrari, and Pininfarina, were increasingly aware of the value of style, comfort and practicality as well as power and performance. It had a bit more space inside, and it was relatively undemanding to drive, without the nervous nature of the race-based cars. It was still quick, though, with a strong 250bhp and a top speed of around 150mph, and it had superb handling, steering and brakes – because it still shared a lot of the latest chassis layout with its more specialised 250 cousins. All of which, again, made it a strong seller, and up to 1964 it added around another 350 sales.

But the other thing that the Lusso would soon become known for was slightly sadder – it was really the last of the 250 road car line. With totally inevitability, Ferrari was ready to move forward again, as Ferrari, amazingly, found a way to squeeze a tiny bit more from the extraordinary Colombo V12, and to create another superb range, the 275s.

BELOW 250LM, 1967

# Chapter 6

# The Rival

FROM 1964, WITH THE END OF THE 250 era, the beginning of the 275s and beyond, Ferrari had another new reason to keep moving forwards – and it was called Lamborghini. As with Ferrari, the marque was named after its founder; and like Enzo Ferrari, Ferrucio Lamborghini knew exactly what he wanted to do with his cars. In Lamborghini's case, it was simple, he wanted to beat Ferrari; and in the beginning, it was personal.

Lamborghini was born barely 20 miles from Ferrari's birthplace, but 21 years later. And so far, his closest connection with the motor industry had been as a tractor manufacturer. Manufacturing domestic and industrial heating and air-conditioning systems, too, he was successful and wealthy, and his taste for supercars had included several Ferraris. But like many other Ferrari owners,

when he had had problems with his cars and tried to resolve them with Enzo directly, he had been treated with something approaching contempt – because to Ferrari, customers were still no more than an irritation that paid for his beloved race cars.

Most of those who Ferrari treated that way just accepted it as part of the mystique; Lamborghini didn't – he vowed instead to create a road car that would beat Ferrari, and he intended to treat his customers rather better, too. He kept his word. At the 1963 Turin Show Lamborghini unveiled the prototype 350 GTV, a car to rival Ferrari's latest 250s in virtually every area. Styled by Scaglione, it looked stunning, and its chassis engineering was as aggressively modern as its looks, including all-round independent suspension where Ferrari's 250s all still had non-independent rear axles.

Its 3.5-litre V12 engine was designed by Giotto Bizzarrini, poached from Ferrari after he had created the legendary 250 GTO, of which more in a moment. Like the rest of the 350GTV, it pointedly out-did its Maranello rivals. It was bigger, at 3.5 litres, it had four cams where the 250s had two, it had much of the sophistication of a racing engine, and in the GTV, with six twin-choke carburettors it had far more power than Ferrari's comparable road cars – with about 360bhp. Even worse news for Ferrari (though he would never have admitted it), within a year Lamborghini had put the car into production, as the 350GT, only slightly toned-down, so still with a Ferrari beating 280bhp, and with styling by Touring.

The newcomer was almost universally greeted as a real challenge to Ferrari, and even Enzo must have recognised its

technical brilliance. But in one way it had a positive effect on its rival – it obliged Ferrari to respond. Hence the introduction of the 275 family, in 1964.

At that year's Paris Show (Ferrari's longtime venue of choice for major launches), he showed off not one but two cars with the new 275 label (indicating a new capacity of 3.3 litres), and they were identified as the 275 GTB (for Gran Turismo Berlinetta) and 275 GTS (for Gran Turismo Spyder) – in other words, one coupe and one convertible, because whatever else Enzo Ferrari had learned in recent years, he had definitely learned that the market would now buy more than one sort of Ferrari.

Its capacity was still smaller than Lamborghini's 350GT, and it still only had two camshafts, but the GTB matched the 350GT's 280bhp while the open-topped GTS acknowledged a slightly softer character with its 260bhp state of tune. Spurred by Lamborghini or otherwise, the 275s also arrived with the independent rear suspension the 250 never had, which also let him mount the gearbox at the back as a 'transaxle', improving the balance and making the new 275 the best handling Ferrari road car so far, and one of the quickest. Pointedly, too, Ferrari offered a higher-tuned 300bhp version, various light-weight body panels, and aerodynamic tweaks to reduce front-end lift for any customer with competitive leanings – while from the start, Lamborghini showed no interest in racing at all.

And that, of course, was a really big difference between the Italian supercar rivals, especially at this stage in the 1960s when Ferrari was rampant in sports car racing in particular – and the road car based 250 family had reached

BELOW 275 GTB Longnose, 1966

its peak with the natural successor to the 250GT SWB, the stunning 250GTO, which remains one of Ferrari's greatest cars ever.

Nominally, it was an evolution of the SWB, but like more than one Ferrari it took a broad view of the racing rules that supposedly laid down what was permissible. To suit the rules, it was nominally a road car, and sold as such – but it clearly bent the rule that said 100 examples must be made to be eligible for racing. Ferrari argued that the SWB satisfied that part of the rules and that the GTO was only an evolution of that, and the authorities, amazingly, accepted the argument – possibly because Ferrari was as important to the sport as the sport was to Ferrari.

And to some extent the GTO was an evolution of the SWB, but it also went way beyond that. The chassis was heavily modified with extra tubing that was supposedly only there to support the body but which clearly made the car much stiffer. The engine was a 300bhp version of the full—race Testa Rossa V12, which was acceptable for a racing 250 – but it was set further back, lower down and with a new five-speed gearbox, all of which the authorities accepted as 'evolution'.

Most obvious of all, it had a completely new shape, devised in the wind tunnel by the GTO's chief engineer, Bizzarrini. Again, the rules said 'evolution'; again Ferrari got away with completely new. And in this case it was dominated by the new emphasis on low drag, low-lift aerodynamics, which were becoming just as important as outright power as speeds continued to rise. Even as a 'road car', it had no bumpers, virtually no trim, plastic in every window except the windscreen, not even a

*ABOVE* 250 GTO interior, 1963

speedometer. Amazingly the rule makers accepted Ferrari's 'SWB evolution' argument, gave the new car the 'O for Omologato' label, and in 1962 GT became GTO.

Just 39 were built up to 1964, and a 250 GTO can now sell for millions of pounds, but in their day they were simply Ferrari's most effective racing GT cars. From 1962 to 1964 the GTO won a hat-trick of sports car world championships and literally hundreds of races. But as the rear-engined revolution approached it was also the end of an era.

# Chapter 7

# Motorsport

WHILE ALL THIS HAD BEEN happening, Ferrari had had a remarkable few years on the racing front. In sports car racing, the importance of the Le Mans 24-Hour race had attracted the attention of American giant Ford, who had decided that winning the great race would do wonders for their road car sales, worldwide. But having no experience in building European type sports racing cars, in the early 1960s they attempted to take a short-cut by trying to buy Ferrari! Ferrari said no, however, and while Ford would eventually build their own racing department and win several times at Le Mans with the GT40 and its successors, Ferrari took great satisfaction from resisting the big-budget Ford steam-roller until 1966.

As we've seen, Ferrari won at Le Mans every year from 1960 to 1965, but that 1965 win for Jochen Rindt and Masten Gregory with a privately entered 275LM would be Ferrari's last in the world's greatest endurance race, as first Ford, then Porsche, Renault and Matra started

ABOVE Enzo Ferrari
with Gendebien during
Grand Prix trials at
Monza, 1959

OPPOSITE Wolfgang
von Trips getting into
car at the Italian Grand
Prix, 1961

to dominate. They didn't give up without a fight, in the prototype category Porsche took the title from Ferrari in 1964, Ferrari won it back in 1965, Porsche won in 1966 and Ferrari again in 1967 – but after that it was Porsche and Ford all the way in the prototypes. Even more surprisingly, Ferrari's long run in the GT classes came to an end in 1965 when the Ford-backed Shelby Cobra Daytonas took the GT title (ironically with a car that bent the rules just as much as Ferrari's previously all-conquering 250GTO).

In Grand Prix racing, too, a new era was dawning, and Ferrari would go into it with mixed fortunes – much of the drama being about Enzo's famous insistence on doing things his own way. His attitude towards putting the engine behind the driver had been neatly summed up by the way he had run the Ferrari Formula 1 effort through the end of the 1950s and into the 1960s – mainly swimming against the tide, as ever.

Hawthorn had won the 1958 championship for Ferrari with the front-engined Dino 246F1, and while Ferrari had a revised car, the 256F1, for 1959, with both Hawthorn and Collins dead he fumbled over drivers. He ran no fewer than seven during the season, and they weren't bad drivers, but they only scored two points between them.

The real problem, though, was less about the drivers than about the cars. By 1959, spurred by Cooper, the rear-engined revolution had already started, and in 1960 (the last year of the 2.5-litre Formula 1) Ferrari stuck to the front-engined layout while virtually every other team put the power behind the driver – for far better packaging, better handling, and less aerodynamic drag. Ferrari meanwhile pursued his theory that power was everything (and he did build very good engines) and again paid the price, with just one 1960 Grand Prix win, for Phil Hill at Monza.

was ready from Day One and the new shark-nosed 156 was not only powerful (and beautiful) it was mid-engined, too.

Stirling Moss won for Cooper and Lotus respectively in Monaco and at the Nurburgring, but Ferrari (aside from missing the US Grand Prix) won everything else. There wasn't as much celebration as there should have been, though. Phil Hill won the drivers' title after team-mate Wolfgang von Trips was killed at Monza – where he could have clinched the championship himself. Fourteen spectators were also killed in the accident, and for the next few years Formula 1 became a pitched battle between Ferrari and the new British teams, notably Cooper, Lotus and BRM – but now with the British usually on top. Ferrari did have one notable success though, when former motor cycle racer John Surtees won the 1964 world championship, and in doing so became the first (and still the

For 1961, though, he turned the tables, as the new 1.5-litre Formula 1 arrived. This time it was mainly his English rivals who held back, hoping the start of the new formula would be delayed until they had their new designs ready. So while they mainly arrived with half developed cars and engines, Ferrari only) man ever to win a world championship on both four wheels and two. But it would be Ferrari's last Formula 1 title for quite some time.

Away from the racing circus, across the Atlantic, where the big V12s were still the Ferrari of choice for many, another change was coming, too, after Ferrari had upped the stakes one more time with a new model whose name said all you needed to know – the 500 Superfast. Like the new 275 family it arrived in 1964, and had evolved from the 410 Superamerica via some spectacular Pininfarina concept cars. In 1956 (when they were still Pinin Farina) they transformed an early Superamerica

ABOVE John Surtees testing F1 prototype, 1962

into a stunning blue and white Paris Show car called the Superfast, with a cantilevered roofline, wraparound glass and flamboyant fins – plus 380bhp under the long bonnet, from the 410 competition car. In 1957 they had showed the 4.9 Superfast, with the same power but a conventional roof and no fins, while the very sleek Superfast II followed in 1960, based on

the 4-litre 400 Superamerica that had replaced the 410 the year before. That in turn went through two more styling evolutions in 1962, as Superfasts III and IV – until the genuine article, the production 500 Superfast, was unveiled at the Geneva Show in March 1964, and aimed, like most of the big V12-engined Ferraris before it, squarely at power-hungry America.

The numbering had a different meaning and here stood for 5 litres, which was the biggest engine Ferrari had yet built, and remained so for a very long time. With 400bhp, it was also the most powerful road car Ferrari had built, and amazingly, it would be for another 20 years. It had all disc brakes and a five-speed gearbox, but it still had non-independent rear suspension, and a top speed of anything up to 160mph. It also had the power to carry a lot of luxurious wood and leather trim and it was a superb long distance grand tourer,

if a bit big for a town car. They only sold 36, but the customers included Peter Sellers, the Aga Khan and the Shah of Persia, who could all afford a Ferrari costing twice the price of Rolls Royce at the time, and one of the most expensive cars in the world.

But while it was the biggest and fastest of the American-focussed 'big-block' cars of the time, it wasn't quite the last. That was very different, and introduced in 1966 just as the Superfast was drifting out of production. It was the 365 California cabriolet, and it wasn't one of either Ferrari's or Pininfarina's best. Its styling was over-fussy, it was heavy, and with 4.4 litres it had 'only' 320bhp. They built just fourteen up to 1967, but by that time Ferrari had more attractive alternatives. Which takes us neatly back to the 275 bloodline, and signs of new thinking.

Threatened by Lamborghini or not, the first 275s were hugely successful cars for Ferrari, the GTB selling more than 450 and the GTS around 200. In 1966 there had even been a short-lived and very rare spin-off intended for racing customers, the 275GTB/C (for Competizione), which was almost as flagrant a rule-bender as the 250 GTO before it. But even as it made its brief appearance, the next developments were on their way.

And again, Ferrari covered more than one possible direction, for pure road car customers and for those he really preferred, who might indulge an interest in competition, too, as the lines split.

BELOW 275 GRB Competizione Speciale, 1965

# Chapter 8

# The Simple Direction

THE SIMPLER DIRECTION STARTED when the 275 line was succeeded (logically enough) by the 330s, starting with the 330 GTC coupe in 1966 and followed a few months later by the 330 GTS Spyder. Or not quite, because before that

there had been a 4-litre 330 America late in 1963 and a similarly-powered but 250-based 330 GT 2+2 early in 1964, before the independently-sprung 275 was unveiled. The 2+2 at least was a big sales success but with its old-fashioned chassis it was a dead end, while the 'real' 275-based 330s were another genuine new beginning.

Those 1966 coupe and spyder newcomers were sisters under the skin with chassis further developed beyond the 275's. And with 4 litres and 300bhp they were good for between 145 and 150mph with great refinement and excellent road manners as the GTS became Ferrari's best selling soft-top to date. That was a bit of a swansong, though, as worries about threatened safety legislation in America made Ferrari think twice about the future of open cars – which needed the American market if

they were to have any chance of commercial success. So there would be a
365GTS spyder in 1968, but like the 365
California, it was short-lived, and aside
from the very rare Daytona Spyder these
would be Ferrari's last significant soft-
top production models for many years.

The coupes had no such worries
about legislation, and went from
strength to strength, again with a twist,
in the shape of the 275 GTB/4 line,
which alongside the softer new 330s was

the 275 development for the buyer with
competition interests. The '4' was the
clue to what made it different – finally
revealing Ferrari's first four-cam road
car engine, at least partly in response to
Lamborghini. It was a gem, with
300bhp and a top speed well over
150mph, but remarkably it was just as
flexible and driver-friendly as the 'ordinary' two cam 275s, and a brilliant fore-
runner to the legendary Daytona –
which is where the 330 line led next.

ABOVE 330 GTC,
1965-67
OPPOSITE 330 GTS,
1967

ABOVE 365 Spyder
California, 1967

First there was the 4.4-litre 320bhp 365GT 2+2 in 1967, and the inevitable 365GTC and GTS models, but alongside them was something else.

This was not only one of the all-time great Ferraris, it was one that proved once and for all that whatever anyone else did, Ferrari was Ferrari. By the time it was introduced, in 1968, as Ferrari's flagship road car and the most expensive one he'd built so far, any serious racing car (even Ferrari's, though he'd resisted longer than most) was mid-engined. And Lamborghini had stunned the exotic car world by launching to mid-engined Miura in 1966. Even Ferrari had just announced the smaller mid-engined 206GT Dino, albeit without Ferrari badging. But the mighty Daytona, with typical Ferrari stubbornness, would have the engine in the front.

It wasn't such a throwback as it might

have sounded, though. With all Ferrari's expertise, the Daytona was truly a masterpiece.

Named for the American racing venue, its real name was 365GTB/4, which in true Ferrari fashion tells you all you need to know: 365 for 4.4 litres, GTB for Gran Turismo Berlinetta, and 4 for the number of camshafts. It was styled, stunningly, by Pininfarina and wasn't much bigger than a 275GTB/4. But it was way more powerful, with 352bhp, which significantly also just beat the 350bhp Miura. Almost more important than the power, though, was the character. The Daytona was massively fast, with a top speed of 174mph and 0-60mph in 5.4 seconds (which is impressive nearly forty years on). But it was also ultra-flexible and relaxing to drive, and just as Ferrari had intended it was a true grand tourer, capable of eating up hundreds of miles in considerable comfort, where its mid-engined rival was more exotic but far less easy to live with. With the engine set way back

LEFT 365 GTB4, 1968

for near perfect weight distribution, it even had the handling to frighten the tail-heavy Miura – or any other car of its day. And it would be a very long time indeed before anyone built a faster front-engined car.

While Ferrari's road cars were flourishing through the mid 1960s and into the 1970s, though, the racing side was struggling again, and for once they seemed short of answers. A new 3-litre Formula 1 had come into force in 1966, and this time it was Enzo who wasn't as

prepared as he thought he was, and the opposition was ready to take advantage.

Ferrari, to be fair, had started in apparently good shape with the all-new V12-powered 312 Grand Prix car; but Surtees, having taken a last win for Ferrari in the 1966 Belgian Grand Prix, left the team only a few weeks later, after arguments about Ferrari's entry into the Le Mans race. Then there was even worse news as Lorenzo Bandini was killed when his car crashed in flames in the Monaco Grand Prix early in 1967.

Thereafter, in spite of the talents of drivers such as Jacky Ickx, Chris Amon and Clay Regazzoni, Ferrari struggled badly through the early part of the 3-litre formula, while first Brabham, then Lotus, Tyrrell, the French Matras and eventually McLaren in turn dominated the championship. And while Ferrari picked up the odd race win, Formula 1 titles continued to elude them.

Alongside the racing and the mainstream road car activity, Ferrari explored two very different directions, too – one of which didn't take him far, while the other laid the foundations for a branch that eventually became the strongest of all. The route that didn't grab the imagination (although it actually included some fine cars) was the larger, more saloon-like 2+2 family that

**BELOW** Ferrari P4, driven by Lorenzo Bandini and Chris Amon, 1967

started with the 365GT/4 2+2 in 1972; the one that made Ferrari a far bigger company than it could ever have been with big cars alone started a bit earlier, with the original V6-powered Dino road car, named like the Dino race engines for the son Ferrari had lost.

Alongside the Daytona, there had been a 365GTC/4, which shared the same engine but with slightly less power (about 320bhp) a softer character and a bit more space – and the 365GT/4 2+2 (unveiled, inevitably, in Paris) was the first Ferrari where the +2 was more than token, a car that was meant to appeal to a new kind of customer who wanted space (possibly for a growing family) and comfort (maybe for long distance touring) as well as Ferrari-like performance.

Styled by Pininfarina, it still only had two doors, but it was wider and roomier than the 365GT 2+2, on a longer wheelbase but in a package that was no longer overall, thanks to shorter nose and tail overhangs. With the four-cam 4.4-litre V12 that gave it the '4' in its name, it had 320bhp, a top speed of 150mph, good handling and genuine practicality. As such it paved the way for several 2+2 successors, starting with the super-elegant

400 GT, launched in 1976, which took size and power to 4.8 litres and 340bhp respectively – and even offered another extraordinary revolution for Ferrari, the option of automatic transmission!

The line continued with the fuel-injected 310bhp 400i from 1979 (injection replacing carburettors mainly to help comply with new emissions rules, hence the drop in power), and from 1985 the 412 – essentially still the same, crisp Pininfarina shape but now almost 5 litres, with 340bhp again, and more modern touches including anti-lock brakes. But when that went out of production in 1989, after almost 3000 2+2 of one sort or another had been built since the first 375 GT4 2+2, Ferrari steered away from the ersatz saloon market for quite a long time.

As for the Dinos and beyond, they merit a chapter of their own. . .

BELOW F 400i, 1981

# Chapter 9

# Dino

WITH THE NAME DINO, Ferrari did two things that he needed to do: he honoured the name of the son who had died so young, and he gave himself the opportunity to create a series of cars that at the time, good as they were, he wouldn't have been entirely comfortable to call Ferrari. But while they didn't at first carry the Ferrari badge, the early Dinos were without a doubt amongst the most significant cars Ferrari ever made.

The first Dino road car, like the first Dino racers, was a car that broke the Ferrari mould. It didn't have twelve cylinders in the front, it had six in the back, and it was smaller and less powerful than any road car he'd built in a very long time. But it was modern, it was brilliant, and it was the start of the direction that Ferrari would soon take much further.

It had its real origins not with Dino himself (who had died in 1956, remember) but in a Pininfarina styling exercise labelled the Dino Berlinetta which appeared at the Paris Show in 1965, plus another called the Dino Berlinetta

GT (shown in Turin in 1966), and a third, which was all but a production-ready Dino in Turin again in 1967 – before the real thing appeared in the middle of 1968 as the full-production Dino 206GT.

It did have a racing connection, too – to build a 1.6-litre V6 engine in sufficient numbers to qualify for the new Formula 2 racing regulations, just as Dino the son had conceived his V6 for an earlier Formula 2.

To make the numbers, Ferrari would actually have to enter a partnership with Fiat to use the same V6 in a series of less exotic and much cheaper front-engined sports cars (which appeared as the Pininfarina-bodied Fiat Dino spyder and the Bertone-bodied Fiat Dino coupe in 1966). But even that had far reaching

OPPOSITE Dino badge, 1968

BELOW Pininfarina's Dino Competition concept, 1967

consequences as it paved the way for Fiat taking commercial control of Ferrari in 1969 while leaving Enzo himself to concentrate on his real love, racing.

The Dino V6 engine, though, was a pure Ferrari design, and in its way as brilliant as many of the apparently far more exotic V12s. It was the third generation of Dino V6, and the first one for a road car. It had a 65 degree vee angle and four camshafts, and while the rac-

ing versions had to be 1.6 litres, the roadgoing capacity was 2 litres. Its compactness and light weight were the keys to packaging it into a mid-engined road car where Ferrari had so far resisted doing anything so adventurous with the much bigger, much heavier V12s. So the Pininfarina-styled road car was small, and even more beautiful than the show cars that pre-dated it. The styling was clever, too – especially that 'flying buttress' rear window design that was a neat solution to getting air into the rear engine bay while still leaving space for a rear window, and reasonable visibility.

And the mechanical packaging was brilliant. The engine was mounted transversely with the gearbox and final drive unit behind (or if you thought of the normal line of the engine, alongside). It gave 180bhp at first, and it wasn't very reliable – with cam-chain, valve and overheating problems (which tended to blow head gaskets), but it was quick for its size, and with racing style all-wish-

BELOW 246 Dino buttress

bone, all-independent suspension and such light weight, it had outstanding handling and agility. It didn't have a Ferrari badge anywhere to be seen (it was simply badged Dino), but there was nothing about it that wasn't worthy of the Ferrari name.

But it got better. They only built about 150 Dino 206GTs before it took a classically Ferrari route and in 1969 turned into the Dino 246GT. Which had a 2.4-litre stretch of the four-cam V6 that was not only usefully more powerful with 195bhp but was a lot more reli-

able, too. It was also more flexible at low speeds, which made the Dino 246GT easier to drive, and as such more appealing to an even wider audience – at a price that opened 'Ferrari' ownership to a market it had never had before.

Even beyond that, there were huge achievements. The 246GT and a GTS spyder version sold strongly right through to 1974, with around 4000 cars built in that time, while the Fiat Dinos had lasted until 1972 adding their own sales success. The more people drove them, the more special they realised they were. And the Dino V6's cousins even achieved some extraordinary competition successes – away from just racing. The engine powered the Lancia Stratos to three successive World Championships for Makes in international rallying, in 1974, 1975 and 1976 – and sensationally, won the Monte Carlo Rally as late as 1979, when Lancia's experimental turbocharged version of the engine could give as much as 350bhp.

Not least, the Dino changed the commercial face of Ferrari. Its production volume meant adding a new 100,000 square foot extension to the Maranello works. And in 1969 Fiat assumed the role of proprietor. Back in 1960, the original Auto Avio Costruzione had finally been renamed Societa Esercizio Fabbriche Automobili e Corse (SEFAC) Ferrari. Now Enzo sold fifty per cent of the company to Fiat, relieving him of worries about road car production while leaving him in complete charge of the racing side – which to Enzo himself was clearly the dream situation. And it was largely made possible by the car named for the son he still mourned. So the Dino may have been a small car, but its influence was huge.

**BELOW** Lancia Stratos - Dino-engined Lancia rally car, 1973

# Racing Philosophy

365 GT4 Boxer, 1974

WHILE FERRARI'S MODEL LINE HAD moved on from the last 250 to the Daytona and Dino generation, Ferrari's racing philosophy, as we have seen, had taken a new avenue that was about to have an even bigger influence on the next generation of Ferrari road cars. In racing, after some initial but futile resistance, Ferrari had finally joined the mid-engined revolution with his Grand Prix and sports car racers in the early 1960s, while stubbornly keeping the prancing horses firmly in front of the cart for his road cars - even when other rivals, and especially newcomer Lamborghini, had already brought the mid-engined layout to the road, on the surface of it making even Ferrari's greatest offerings look oddly old-fashioned.

Which wasn't true, of course, because many of Ferrari's mid-engined rivals were as flawed as a car like the Daytona was brilliant. But even Ferrari couldn't swim against the tide forever, and at the Paris Salon in 1973 he finally took the big step, with the 365GT4/BB – the replacement for the much-loved Daytona, and Ferrari's first big mid-engined road car.

As with the Daytona, the 365, GT and 4 bits signified 4.4 litres, four cams and Gran Turismo. As before, one of the Bs stood for Berlinetta, too – but the other now stood for 'Boxer', and that indicated just as big a change from the Ferrari norm as the new mid-engine layout. Because it revealed the change from the

classic V12 to a 'flat-12' layout with horizontally-opposed pistons, just like the flat-six Porsche 911.

As with mid engines, Ferrari had already used the 'flat' cylinder layout in motor sport – with mixed results. In Grand Prix racing, the first generation Ferrari flat-12s showed a lot of promise but not much else. In sports car racing, though, Ferrari bounced back in 1972 with a prototype racer also powered by the flat-12 engine, and largely based on the 3-litre Formula 1 cars. This was the

**ABOVE** 365 GT4 BB engine, 1974

312P prototype, and in 1972 it took the sports car title back from Porsche by winning every race it contested – although those, sadly, did not include Le Mans, where Enzo Ferrari's love-hate relationship with the organisers was still in full flow.

Ferrari did go to Le Mans in 1974 but was well beaten by Matra, who also took the championship. And although many private entrants carried the Ferrari colours over the next few decades, that was Ferrari's final year as a serious works contender in sports car racing.

But while the mid-engined flat-12 race cars had had both triumphs and disasters, with Fiat now holding the commercial reins it was no coincidence that the road cars were to echo the marque's current racing car philosophies – and that had started, of course, with the mid-engined flat-12 Boxer.

They'd had a while to get used to the idea, since Ferrari showed the BB as a concept car in Turin in 1971, but not everyone readily accepted the Boxer, as it was usually called, as a step in the right direction. More than one magazine immediately pitted it against the Daytona, and not all of them thought the Boxer was better. But Lamborghini had already shown the sensational Countach prototype, and Ferrari had to respond.

What they created was classic Ferrari – almost plain alongside the flamboyant Countach, but superbly engineered, with the genuine race-bred touches that

BELOW Lamborghini Countach, 1980s

ABOVE 365 GT4 BB
interior, 1974

The flat-12 had the same capacity (even the same pistons and rods) as the Daytona and four camshafts – driven for the first time on a Ferrari by toothed belts. With two triple-choke carburettors for each cylinder bank it produced 344bhp, which wasn't quite as much as a Daytona but gave the BB (which was very slightly lighter with less aerodynamic drag) an almost identical 175mph top speed. And although its handling was different from a Daytona's, it was pretty good by any standards – the steering was lighter and it had massive grip, but with the rearward weight bias it was inevitably a bit less forgiving near its limits.

Also on the debit side, it wasn't quite such a practical grand tourer as the roomy Daytona – but it was a success, especially in re-establishing Ferrari as a 'modern' thinker who could still challenge Lamborghini.

And exactly like all its front-engined ancestors, it soon started to evolve, starting with the 5-litre, 360bhp 512BB in 1976, and the final step, the fuel-injected 512Bbi from 1981 – both those evolu-

Lamborghini could never claim. It was clever, too, adapting the conventional mid-engined layout (which has the engine behind the driver but ahead of the transmission and rear axle) to give a more compact package with the gearbox below the wide but shallow engine and the final drive behind. It also mounted the radiator at the front of the car, again distancing Ferrari thinking from the Countach, with its dramatic rear cooling ducts, and improving weight distribution.

tions to make the Boxer easier to drive and more friendly to tougher emissions regulations. Then in 1984, Ferrari showed that mid engines were here to stay when he introduced an all-new successor to the Boxer – the Testarossa.

It was the answer to a major problem that Ferrari could no longer ignore –

developments notwithstanding, the flagship Boxer had never actually satisfied US emissions rules, and so had never been officially sold in America. And while he could sell the smaller V8 models, that was a high-end, high-profit market Ferrari couldn't live without for very long. The Testarossa was the

BELOW Boxer, 1981

answer, and although it wasn't really Enzo's own kind of car, it would have the refinement, driveability, comfort, equipment and most of all the clean engine performance to make it acceptable on the far side of the Atlantic. But Ferrari meant it to have serious performance, too.

It would have a heavily revised version of the four-cam flat-12 engine, now with four-valve cylinder heads and electronic management to attack the emissions problem without sacrificing power. The engine was also significantly lighter, which helped weight distribution, and produced 390bhp, which gave a top speed of around 180mph with the kind of flexibility that made the Testarossa a very user-friendly supercar.

It improved in other ways, too. Those dramatic side vents reveal that the radiators had moved from the nose to behind the doors, keeping the cabin cooler and moving weight to the middle of the car where it would have a less damaging effect on the handling. The brakes were bigger and the clutch action was lighter. There were big aerodynamic gains, too, in the new Pininfarina shape, reducing high-speed lift; and with longer wheelbase, wider tracks and the latest, wider, lower-profile tyres, the Testarossa had more grip and better on-limit manners. To complete the transformation, it had more seating space, more luggage space, more equipment (including standard air-conditioning), and generally a more civilised character all-round. And in case you were wondering, as with the racers, the Testarossa name came from the red-painted cam covers.

And as ever, it evolved, in this case for a full decade – and it sold in big numbers. From 1984 to 1992 the first generation found almost 7200 customers, making it by far the biggest selling 'full-

sized' Ferrari yet. Only then did it need real changes, but when the 512TR was introduced it looked like a Testarossa but it was really almost a completely new car. The nose was a bit more rounded, but the big changes were all under the skin, and especially in that superb flat-12 engine. More cylinder head, inlet and exhaust system and electronic management developments pushed power up to an impressive 421bhp, while delivering cleaner emissions and lower fuel consumption. The 512TR was also lighter, and performance had increased to include a 195mph maximum and 4.5 second 0-60mph time – which put it right back into the sharp end of supercar performance.

**ABOVE** Testarossa rear tail light

The chassis had been uprated in line with the performance – with a better gearbox, quicker steering, even bigger cross-billed brakes, and a lot of suspension tuning. The chassis was stiffer, and most important of all, the engine had been lowered in the chassis, to improve balance. Finally, the comfort and equipment package was improved again, to complete a car that was better than the original in almost every respect.

But even that wasn't quite the end: the final development appeared at the Paris Show in 1994 as the F512M, where the M stood for Modificato, or modified – which is exactly what it was. Power was up again, to 432bhp, and cosmetic changes included new front and rear lights and new wheels. Although it didn't last long, it was a fine Testarossa swansong.

While the bigger cars were the most glamorous, powerful and expensive end of the Ferrari market, though, it would be very wrong to ignore the other string to Ferrari's bow – the smaller, more affordable, larger production families that in effect had started with the original Dino.

We left the first chapter of that story back in the early 1970s, with the 246GT generation and Fiat's arrival as commercial partner for Ferrari – coinciding with much extended production facilities and expanding sales. Clearly, Ferrari wasn't going to let this huge new market slip, and in 1974 the 308GT/4 (which had been previewed in Paris late in 1973) was launched into production. It even, finally, added Ferrari badges alongside the Dino ones. But for once, Ferrari seemed to have slipped up.

By now, virtually every production Ferrari was pure Pininfarina – but this one was styled by Bertone, it was a 2+2, and although it was very neat it was different enough to worry many of Ferrari's surprisingly conservative customers. On the plus side, six cylinders had been replaced by Ferrari's first road-car V8, with four cams, 3 litre capacity and 250bhp, which was enough for 150mph and a useful leap from the 246GT. But although the 308 was a bit bigger and heavier, it was still quick and agile – and it deserved better than the muted welcome it received.

It would survive until 1980 and sold in reasonable numbers, but even before it was phased out, an alternative had been ushered in. And this one was by Pininfarina again - the 308 GTB, and its open-topped cousin the 308 GTS, unveiled in 1978. Though the name had disappeared, it had a lot of the character of the earlier Dinos, including a fall back to a strictly two-seater format – the

twist this time was that the bodywork was in glassfibre, another first for a Ferrari. Or at least it was on the coupe; the spyder was in steel to put back the stiffness lost by losing the roof. And another twist, alongside the two-seater 308s in 1980, they launched a further variation – the 2+2 Mondial 8, based on the 3-litre V8 308s with a stretched wheelbase and higher roofline, styled by Pininfarina but quite distinct from the others, and aimed straight at the market lost with the passing of the Bertone 308 GT/4! By 1983 there would be a Mondial Cabriolet too. It was a complicated few years at Maranello. . .

BELOW Mondial 8, 1981

# Chapter 11

# Model Success

PININFARINA'S V8S comfortably outsold the Bertone GT/4 from the start, hence its early demise, and the 308 family, Mondial included deserved its success. It also showed that Ferrari was now strong enough in this end of the market to make some brave moves. At the top, the 308 gained fuel injection from 1980 (emissions concerns again) as the 308 GTBi and GTSi, then four-valve cylinder heads from 1982 as the GTBqv (and GTSqv) 'quattrovalvole', or four valves – changes which also applied to the Mondials in their turn. The brave part, though, was at the other end of the market, where Ferrari recognised an opportunity in some areas where smaller engined cars had tax advantages. So from 1975 to 1983 they offered 170bhp 2-litre models, as the 208 GT/4, 208 GTB and 208 GTS, which had more modest performance but were still real Ferraris.

From 1982 to 1985 there were turbocharged 208s, too, with most of the performance of the 308's for less money; but at much the same time there would also be a considerably more spectacular spin-off from the smaller

car line, which would be the starting point for several generations of super-Ferrari, right at the top of the range – the 288GTO.

The final link from 308 to 288 was the 328 family that would appear in production in 1985, as the next natural progression of the V8 family, when the four-cam, four-valve engine's capacity grew to 3.2 litres, and power climbed to 270bhp, again across the board of 328GTB, 328GTS and 3.2 Mondials in both coupe and cabriolet shapes. Beyond that, though, the 328 was a very straightforward, faster, more driver-friendly, better equipped evolution of the 308, and just as big a seller.

The 288GTO, on the other hand, was a massively more dramatic development, and its roots were in an area where Ferrari's road cars had had a more tenuous connection for the past few years – in motor sport.

The importance Ferrari placed on this

new car was revealed by the name, which stands for Gran Turismo Omologato, a car homologated for motor sport. This was only the second time Ferrari had ever used the letters; the first was more than twenty years ago, on that greatest of Ferrari classics, the race-bred 250GTO that won a hat-trick of World Sports Car Championships for the marque back in the mid 1960s. And as with the 250GTO, Ferrari's original purpose for the 288GTO was motor sport, where Ferrari had had no direct interest in sports car racing since the mid 1970s.

OPPOSITE 308 GTBi, 1982

BELOW 308 GTBqv, 1984

The other connection was that one word, 'Omologato', which now as then carried the requirement (beyond all the technical definitions) of a fixed number of cars produced in a certain period to qualify for the formula in question. With the 250GTO that had been 100 cars, and Ferrari had side-stepped it with that pretence of the 250GTO being an evolution of the 250GT SWB. With the 288GTO the requirement would be

a minimum of 200 cars built to qualify for the new Group B category that applied in both racing and rallying, and Ferrari would play more by the book.

It was a significant formula that tempted Ferrari back into a category other than Grand Prix racing for the first time in more than a decade, since they had officially walked away from sports car racing. But Ferrari was still well aware of the commercial benefits of

BELOW 208 Turbo, 1980

winning on Sunday to sell cars on Monday. And here, finally, was a racing class that would allow Ferrari to come back into the sports car arena without needing a purpose built racer, at a time when they were having to stretch themselves ever harder to stay competitive in Formula 1 racing.

It was Group B, a class designed precisely to do what it had with Ferrari – to attract manufacturers back into the sport with cars that, in theory at least, could also be used on the road. And the requirement for 200 cars meant any manufacturer would definitely have to sell the majority of what they built as road cars, not full-time racers.

Ferrari saw the chance to compete again at Le Mans (still one of the most prestigious events in the world) with a reasonable chance of winning, and at the same time to sell some highly profitable road cars. And he had the perfect starting point in the emerging 328 models.

In fact, look at a 328GTB and a 288GTO side by side and there's no doubt at all about the relationship, but it's also clear that the GTO is a lot more

(according to an 'equivalency' factor of 1.4) 2857cc with it – and the 288's exact capacity was right on the limit, at 2855cc! It had four cams and four valves per cylinder, of course, and a short stroke that allowed it to rev hard. And it had not one but two turbochargers, with intercoolers, and a wastegate to limit maximum boost according to the rules. In road trim it gave 400bhp, for racing (or rallying) it could give 600bhp or even more.

Then Ferrari attacked the weight of the starting-point 328, using exotic

than just a pumped up 328. The Pininfarina shape is similar, but the GTO's wheelbase is longer and the whole car is wider. Even more basically, the V8 engine in the back is turned through 90 degrees, and mounted longitudinally rather than transversely, in front of a new five-speed transaxle in the classic mid-engined racing layout. Which, with the longer wheelbase, gives a lower centre of gravity, more space, and better accessibility for quick maintenance during racing pit stops.

And although this was a V8 not a V12, it was the most powerful engine Ferrari had ever put into a road car. The 288 label stood for 2.8 litres and eight cylinders, and the capacity was set by the racing rules, which allowed four litres without turbocharging or

materials and construction techniques usually only seen in his Grand Prix cars. So most of the body was in super-light-weight composites like Kevlar, and internally there was a mix of Kevlar and aluminium honeycombs. So even though it was bigger than the 328, even in road trim the 288GTO was about 300lb lighter – which gave it a huge power to weight ratio for colossal straight line performance. What's more, with two small turbochargers it had very little 'turbo-lag', and it had massive power even from very low speeds. It

would hit 60mph in 4.8 seconds, 100mph in just over 10 seconds, and even as a road car had a top speed of 189mph – making it the fastest road car Ferrari had ever built.

But it wasn't only the numbers that made it special, it was the whole concept of basing it on one of the more com-pact models in the range. As a road car it hardly felt any bigger than the 328 (and it was even quite well trimmed and equipped) but it had all that perform-ance. It also had massively effective race-bred brakes and suspension that made it stop and handle as well as it went. It was very special indeed.

In competition, though, it never had the chance to show just how special – but not through any fault of its own. This time, Ferrari legitimately built and sold enough cars to satisfy the rules, but just in time for the rules to change. In rally-ing in particular, the sort of cars and the sort of speeds Group B had created were proving to be just too dangerous. In ral-lying, it brought a brief golden age with

ABOVE 288 GTO engine, 1985

ABOVE F40 pre
production model, 1988

the likes of Audi, Ford, Lancia and Peugeot building the most powerful rally cars ever seen. And in sports car racing it could have put the 288GTO head-to-head with the super-high-tech four-wheel drive Porsche 959, but it never happened. In 1986, after a series

of terrible accidents, the Group B cars were banned, and what should have been Ferrari's sports car racing come-back died with it.

It did lay the foundations, though, for an even more famous Ferrari at the extreme end of the range, whose name

would mark a significant anniversary, as well as being the last Ferrari that Enzo Ferrari himself would ever launch. It was the F40, and its appearance in 1987 would mark the fortieth anniversary for Ferrari as a car builder under his own name.

Enzo, in his ninetieth year, had much to commemorate. His cars had won eight Formula 1 manufacturers' championships, ten drivers' titles, almost 100 grands prix, nine Le Mans wins, and too many other major victories even to start listing. He could also look back on all the classic road cars, from the first 125 to the great 250s, the Daytona, the Dinos, even the hugely successful V8 family. But he promised that the F40 would be 'the best Ferrari ever', and many people thought he was right.

There was another reason why it had to be special, and as with the Lamborghini effect in the early 1960s, that was a spur from another rival - in this case Porsche, whose 959 had proved to be even more exotic and considerably faster than Ferrari's recent 288GTO. Ferrari was determined the F40 was going to take the title back from the German car.

Enzo Ferrari unveiled the F40 in person, to a small gathering of journalists and invited guests in Maranello in July 1987 – as the fastest road car ever, and that included the amazing 959. It was the first road car ever to claim a top speed of more than 200mph (at 201mph it was just a whisker faster than the Porsche), and with the extraordinary 0-60mph time of just 3.5 seconds, which few cars can match almost 20 years on.

But it wasn't just the numbers that made the F40 special, it was its whole character, which was as stripped bare and brutal as the rival 959 was complex and driver-friendly. The Porsche, massively powerful and fast as it was, had four-wheel drive, variable ride-height and damping programmes, a six-

ABOVE F40,1990

speed transmission with adaptable final-drive modes, and considerable comfort and luxury equipment – including top class hi-fi and even air-conditioning. The F40 was a racing car in street clothes. It had rear-wheel drive only, little or no interior trim, certainly none of the 959's electronic aids, not even anti-lock braking. The seats were high-backed racing-style buckets, thinly padded, with no height or back-rake adjustment, and pierced with holes to accept full harness belts. The dash and centre tunnel were trimmed in a grey cloth, but there were no carpets, no electric windows (there was a flap in the driver's side to pay autostrada tolls!), no central locking, or even door handles – just cord pulls in thin skinned doors that weighed only 1.5kg each.

The steel spaceframe strengthened by bonded on composite panels was three times as stiff as a conventional chassis but far lighter and the whole car weighed only 1100kg. It was power without frills.

Even more amazing was the way it looked. Pininfarina (who else?) had penned one of the most spectacular looking supercars of all time, dominated by the flat nose, massive wheelarches, dramatic scoops and vents, the deep front air-dam, and that high-mounted full-width rear wing – with the F40 badges embossed into the end-plates.

It was one of the first road cars that seriously needed (and delivered) top-end race-car aerodynamics. Then there were the race car connections you couldn't see, like all the super-light-weight composite body materials and the exotic engine specification. It was based on the 288GTO's twin-turbo V8, with capacity increased to 2.9 litres and injection and ignition management derived from Ferrari's Formula 1 technology. With 478bhp it was the most powerful production car engine in the world when it was launched, and the F40 was the fastest car. It was also one of the most uncompromising, and that was exactly as Enzo intended.

BELOW Enzo's office, as he left it

# Chapter 12

# End of an Era

IT WOULD BE HIS FINAL PERSONAL contribution to the story. He celebrated his 90th birthday in February 1988, but his health was already failing and he was becoming increasingly frail. He died on 14 August that year, and it's unlikely that the world of either supercars or motor sport will see his like again. He achieved great things, and did absolutely every-thing he did in his own way. He was a dif-ficult man to understand, even more difficult to know personally, but he was hugely respected by almost everyone for his unrivalled achievements, especially in racing. The loss of his son Dino had changed his life completely, and he never truly recovered from it. But he made Ferrari what it was, ensured its long term survival under Fiat even after his death, and branded it with such a powerful per-sonality that long after Enzo himself has gone, Ferrari is still very much Ferrari.

It was almost symbolic that just two weeks after the man who founded the marque died, the Formula 1 team, which by Ferrari standards had been struggling for several seasons, returned to the winner's circle – and even more emotionally they did it at Monza, where the Ferrari faithful, the 'tifosi', never lost their fanaticism.

The slump that had started in the mid 1960s had been as bad as Ferrari had ever experienced. Beyond Bandini's death in 1967, they didn't win a single Grand Prix, and they only won once in 1968, with Jacky Ickx in France as the new Cosworth-engined British cars overwhelmed them. 1969 was another no-win season, 1970 brought three wins for Ickx plus one for team-mate Regazzoni but only second place in the constructors' championship – which meant far more to Ferrari than the drivers' title. Then it got worse again, with only three wins in the next three years – two for Mario Andretti in 1971, and another for Ickx, in Germany, in 1972.

After another clean sheet in 1973 they bounced back slightly in 1974 when Regazzoni won one and a Ferrari newcomer added two more. His name was Niki Lauda, who finished second in his first Grand Prix for Ferrari in Argentina in 1974 and won his fourth, in Spain.

OPPOSITE Enzo Ferrari (1898-1988)

BELOW Clay Regazzoni in a Ferrari 312B in the Italian Grand Prix, 1970

He would go on to score fifteen wins for Ferrari, finally beating the tally set by Ascari back in the 1950s, and Lauda put them back onto the championship winning trail as Ferrari's flat-12 Formula 1 cars finally started to deliver.

Ferrari had now refined the packaging even further with transverse gearboxes in the 312T and 312T2 and Lauda won the championship in 1975 and again in 1977, against some of Formula 1's toughest opposition. It not only gave Ferrari the titles, it gave them self-confidence again, and Ferrari held Lauda in great esteem – especially as his 1977 championship came only a year after he had almost died in a fiery accident at the Nurburgring. Before that he had already won five 1976 Grands Prix. After the accident he was given the last rites in hospital but not only did he not die, before the end of the season he raced again, and went to the final race of the year, in Japan, leading the championship from James Hunt. In terribly wet and dangerous conditions, Lauda pulled out of the race after just a few laps – and by finishing fourth Hunt stole the title. Lauda had done some extraordinarily brave things in 1976, but deciding not to race in Fuji with the title almost won was probably the bravest of all.

In 1978, though, Lauda headed for Brabham and it was Carlos Reutemann and another spectacularly quick newcomer, Gilles Villeneuve, who gave Ferrari five wins between them but couldn't beat Mario Andretti and Lotus in the drivers' and constructors' championships. When Ferrari's next title came it was for neither of those drivers, but for South African Jody Scheckter, who won in 1979, driving alongside Villeneuve (the father of Jacques, who almost twenty years later would win the world title for Williams in 1997 – narrowly beating Ferrari's Michael Schumacher). It was three Grand Prix wins each, but Scheckter had more minor placings.

The 1980s and 1990s, though, were almost universally awful for Ferrari in Grand Prix racing, and Scheckter's championship would be the last for 21 years. The change was rapid, too. There were no wins in 1980, just two for Villeneuve in 1981, then the worst year of all in 1982. Gilles Villeneuve died practicing for the Belgian Grand Prix in May and his team-mate Didier Pironi (with whom Villeneuve had had a huge

falling out just before he died) was terribly injured in another practice crash, in Germany. But Villeneuve's replacement, Patrick Tambay, at least raised spirits a little by winning that race at Hockenheim.

They did win the constructors' title (with Tambay and Rene Arnoux driving) in 1983, and another newcomer, Michele Alboreto, won one race in 1984 with the 126C4 – but they'd had three more fairly unproductive years in the last three years of Enzo's life – which saddened him greatly.

So Ferrari headed into the 1990s without the man himself, but in sound commercial health as part of the Fiat empire and pushing forwards as strongly as ever. And the first car to be launched after Ferrari's death proved the point. It was the 348, which replaced the 328 late in 1989 and as normal split opinions between those who thought any change at all must be a change for the worse, and the more realistic ones who recognised that it's what Ferrari always did.

The strictly two-seater 348 (and the 3.4-litre 2+2 Mondial T that first appeared a few months before it) continued the 'entry-level' V8 range (with the usual coupe or spyder alternatives) and brought it right up to date, in the broader market that actually keeps the brand alive. It was a direct descendant of the 308 and 328 line, and in the spirit of the original Dinos, but it was virtually all-new, and thoroughly modern. Driven by what the market wanted, it had become even more sophisticated, more practical and comfortable, and easier to live with – but it had also grown more powerful and quicker. Its totally new styling (by Pininfarina) was smooth, even elegant – and not unlike a scaled-down Testarossa. It was wider, and on a longer wheelbase, for more room inside and a better ride, but with tight packaging it was shorter overall and very handsome. It had many Fiat-sourced details inside, for cost control, but you couldn't mistake if for anything other than a Ferrari either visibly or dynamically.

Like the F40, but to a much lesser degree, of course, it resisted too many frills and promised a purely driver-focussed character. The new number said the V8 was up to 3.4 litres, and naturally with four camshafts and four valves per cylinder. 300bhp was an increase, and took top speed to around 165mph, but more important for the 1990s Ferrari driver, it had even more flexibility across all speed ranges, making it more relaxing to drive without sacrificing the outer limits performance.

**BELOW** Mondial T, 1990

ABOVE The F355, successor to 348

the basis for classic wishbone suspension.

So this first Ferrari after Ferrari hadn't changed directions, it had just continued them, and proved above all that the heritage was safe. What's more, the familiar evolutions continued, too, with the F355 taking over from the 348 in 1994 introducing a dramatically new Pininfarina body style, and a whole catalogue of new technical features that made this one of the biggest leaps Ferrari had taken in a very long time. Its chassis introduced variable damping control, power assisted steering, more rubber on the road and improved aerodynamics all to make the F355 a bit less nervous around its limits than the 348 had been – again recognising that nowadays, not every Ferrari driver was a closet racer.

Like the 288GTO its engine was mounted longitudinally and lower in the chassis (where all its predecessors had had transverse engines), but with a transverse gearbox to make the overall packaging very compact and to give superb handling balance. Given the numbers these cars were now sold in, the chassis was no longer the old multitube affair but a more production-friendly fabricated unit – but that was no problem as it was much stiffer and

Not that performance was compromised, of course. The F355 offered a racing-style paddle gearshift for the manual gearbox. And the four-cam V8 also received its share of new technologies beyond the small capacity increase – including an increase in valve-count to five per cylinder (indicated by the final 5 in the type number), individual throttle controls and titanium conrods. All of which meant it produced 375bhp – or more power per litre than any other non-turbocharged production engine in the world, which was something Enzo Ferrari would have been proud of. So while the F355 was more comfortable and better equipped again, it was also much quicker with headlines of

183mph and 0-60mph in 4.7 seconds. And when the Spyder joined the coupe and the targa-topped GTS it was a very handsome full convertible with an electrically-powered soft-top.

Over in the larger car line, meanwhile, Ferrari after Enzo Ferrari's death had taken a dramatically new direction that you couldn't help thinking he would have approved of – in a new line of front-engined grand tourers that were just as revolutionary in their way as the switch to mid engines had been a couple of decades earlier.

BELOW F355, 1994

# Chapter 13

# Supercars

WHEN FERRARI INTRODUCED THE 456GT in 1993, they turned conventional supercar thinking around – more or less literally. They'd been quite late joining the mid-engined revolution, with the Boxer in 1973, by which time other rivals already had well-established mid-engined credentials. But once they'd joined the club they hadn't made a front-engined car since. Twenty years on, the 456GT was about to change all that.

It was a brave move, not so much in engineering terms but in marketing ones, to say that a front-engined super-car could once again take on what had become the mid-engined mainstream at their own game. And not only to take them on but in many respects to beat them – but that was still what Ferrari was best at, doing things their own way, however unconventional it seemed.

It was an odd situation, but the idea was that the 456GT would be a great grand tourer because it was front-engined, not in spite of it, by going back to the basics of packaging and bringing them right up to date. Not least, among the truly fast cars of the early 1990s, it would be unique – and Ferrari hoped that that would make it attractive to the market, too.

In a way it was clearly from the Daytona bloodline, even down to hints of the Daytona shape and proportion in the Pininfarina lines, but the 456GT had

another 25 years of technical thinking under its skin, too.

The easiest bit to understand was the power: classic supercar thinking, of course – a 5.5-litre four-cam 48-valve V12 with all the latest electronic management advantages, plus a lightweight compactness that showed how far engine design had progressed in a quarter of a century. It delivered 442bhp, which was enough to give the 456GT a top speed of 193mph and 0-60mph in less than five seconds, but just as

important it gave it that refinement and laid-back long-distance flexibility that had become so much a part of the modern Ferrari character – as happy in town or pottering about the country-side as on a transcontinental dash.

The packaging supported that, as a true GT car. It was a 2+2, and roomy enough in the back even for two adults over shorter distances. It was easy to climb into, through big doors, easy to see out of (in a way that few mid-engined cars could be), through big windows. It had decent luggage space, and it was very comfortable and well equipped – clearly designed for long distances at high average speeds. It had all-electric

ABOVE F550 Maranello interior, 1997

With the engine set way back in the super-stiff shell, the gearbox and final drive at the back to help balance it, and with electronically controlled damping that offered comfort, standard and sports levels of stiffness plus self levelling at the rear, it offered a fine combination of ride comfort, handling and refinement. And one more advantage, it was much more forgiving around its limits than the typical, tail-dominated mid-engined car of similar size and power. Incredible as it seemed, Ferrari had genuinely reinvented the classic grand tourer.

Having done that with the touring-biased 2+2 456GT, they took the revolution a stage further when they introduced the next big Ferrari, the 550 Maranello, in 1996. Like the 456GT it was front-engined, but this one was a pure two-seater, and much more biased towards pure performance – which would soon be reflected in a hugely successful sports car racing career for the

seat adjustment, seat heating, air-conditioning, top level sound system, and acres of leather. It was easy to drive in a way the Daytona never was, with power steering, an all-syncromesh six-speed transmission, anti-lock brakes, even a hydraulically-assisted clutch.

new car. The design brief set the scene: 'a car able to meet the needs of Ferrari customers looking for driving emotions and exciting performance, who do not want to forego driveability or comfort', it said. 'Customers attracted by state-of-the-art technical proposals from a company which has always treated design as an aesthetic solution to the demand for performance, and has always built its cars with sophisticated craftsmanship. . .' And this car would top Ferrari's mainstream range.

It looked bigger than the 456GT but it was actually smaller and lighter. And although it had basically the same 5.5-litre V12, variable geometry inlet and exhaust layouts and lighter internal components gave it even more power – with 485bhp to the 456's 442. It's claimed maximum was 199mph, with 60mph in just 4.5 seconds and 100mph in 10.2. It was very fast indeed, and thanks to the same thinking about engine and gearbox layout it was as impeccably balanced as its front-engined cousin – which had already been acclaimed as one of the best handling of all

1990s supercars, whichever end their engine was. The difference, though, was that the 550 was designed to be even more agile and sharp-handling than the 456, with stiffer suspension, even a quicker steering ratio. The standard traction control could be switched off (completely or partly), and race-type underbody aerodynamics gave exceptional high-speed stability. Even more

BELOW F550 Maranello engine, 1999

than the 456GT, perhaps, it showed just what was possible with the classic front-engined layout – and one thing it offered that the 456 never did was an open-topped option in the rare Barchetta.

In 2002 it evolved into the 575 Maranello, with a full 500bhp, the option of paddle-shift manual transmission, further improved suspension, and an even more complete perform-

ance and handling package.

The 500 and 575 family also put Ferrari back on the sports car racing map on a regular basis, competing with several private teams, and winning, in the GT category against the likes of Corvette and Viper.

Ferrari's fortunes at the pinnacle of motor sport, in Formula 1, had also finally taken a huge turn for the better after Ferrari's longest ever spell in the

BELOW The G.P.C. Sport Ferrari 575 Maranello at Silverstone, 2005

Grand Prix racing wilderness since we left the story in 1984.

From that unexpected win in the constructors' championship in 1983, they were about to nose dive again and although they'd finished second in the 1984 series (helped by several points scoring finishes from Rene Arnoux) they'd only scored the single win with Alboreto. He also won two in 1985, in Canada and Germany with the all-new 158-85 car, and although Arnoux won nothing that was enough to give Alboreto runner-up spot in the drivers'

championship and Ferrari second in the constructors', which was probably more than they deserved. Neither Alboreto nor new team-mate Stefan Johansson won anything in 1986 with the 158-86 evolution of the Grand Prix car, but Johansson's replacement Gerhard Berger did win in Japan and Australia right at the end of 1987.

Berger added just one more win for the team in 1988, but at least did it in the best place, at Monza, right on Ferrari's doorstep. Then in 1989 Ferrari signed Briton Nigel Mansell to drive

**ABOVE** Alain Prost
celebrates victory in the
French Grand Prix, 1990

three times with McLaren by taking five wins in his Ferrari debut year (in Brazil, Mexico, Britain and Spain – plus France, which was Ferrari's hundredth Grand Prix victory). Mansell, overshadowed for once, won just one, in Portugal.

Even that, though, wasn't enough to give either Prost or Ferrari a title in 1990, and remarkably Prost never won for the team again, even though he didn't leave until the end of 1992, by which time Mansell had gone, too.

**ABOVE** Alain Prost celebrates victory in the French Grand Prix, 1990

alongside Berger and for a while it looked as though they might have turned the corner. Mansell won two races in his first Ferrari season, in Brazil and Hungary, and Berger won in Portugal. But while three wins was good by Ferrari's recent standards, it was nowhere near enough to put them back into title contention, because as 1990 showed, winning in Formula 1 was tougher than ever.

That was the year Alain Prost joined Mansell at Maranello, and showed why he had already been world champion

New drivers Jean Alesi and Ivan Capelli (replaced late in the season by Nicola Larini) scored only 21 points between them that year, and Alesi and Berger added no more wins in 1993, while the following two years brought the team just one more win in each – from Berger in Germany in 1994 (the year totally overshadowed by the death of Ayrton Senna) and Alesi in Canada in 1995. But another big change was coming.

In 1996, Ferrari signed another new driver, and arguably the greatest they had ever had – Michael Schumacher. He had already won back to back championships with Benetton in the previous two years, and was the perfect choice to restore Ferrari's fortunes, with his mixture of exceptional speed, great development ability, and total commitment.

Even for a talent like Schumacher, though, and new team-mate Eddie Irvine, it was a tough job because Ferrari had fallen so badly behind.

He won three races in 1996, in Spain, Belgium and Italy, helping Ferrari back to second place in the constructors' championship. And he took the title fight to the last round in 1997, battling with Jacques Villeneuve, driving for Williams. Schumacher had won in Monaco, Belgium, Canada, France and Japan, but crashed out of the title-deciding European Grand Prix in Jerez while trying to hold off Villeneuve's clearly faster Williams. It was a controversial end to the season, as Villeneuve's third place gave him the drivers' cham-

BELOW Schumacher leads the way at Jerez, 1997

team another last-round shoot-out, this
time against McLaren's Mika Hakkinen
in Japan. But an extraordinary race that
saw Schumacher stall on the grid, start
from last place, claw his way up to third
then suffer a dramatic puncture – leaving the race win to Hakkinen and
another runners-up slot for Schuey.

It was another Hakkinen and McLaren
year in 1999, and again hounded all the
way by Ferrari, but this time it was Irvine
who came to closest to taking the title
back to Maranello as Schumacher missed
half the season having badly injured his
legs in a first corner accident at
Silverstone in July. Irvine had actually
won the first race, in Australia, and
before his accident Schumacher had won
in Imola and Monaco. With Schumacher
sidelined, Irvine won again in Austria,
and in Germany (where he was waved
through by stand-in team-mate Mika
Salo, who had been leading the race!).
Schuey was back for just the two final
races of the season, and at the first, in
new venue Malaysia, he shadowed the
victorious Irvine with second place. For
the third year in succession, the championship went to the last round with a
Ferrari driver in contention, but this year
it was Irvine! Neither he nor Schumacher

pionship and Schumacher was stripped
of the runner-up position allegedly for
trying to take Villeneuve out.

Six more wins from Schumacher in
1998 (Argentina, Canada, France, Great
Britain, Hungary and Monza) gave the

could catch Hakkinen in Suzuka, though, and with Schuey second Eddie took third – a tantalising four points short of what would have been one of the biggest title upsets in a very long time indeed. For the first time since 1983, though, Ferrari did win the constructors' championship, as the tide turned.

For the next five years, Schumacher and Ferrari (plus an ideal new team-mate in Rubens Barichello) put together a run of Grand Prix domination that hadn't been seen in a very long time, starting with a winning double in 2000 when Schumacher finally beat Hakkinen to the drivers' title to add to

BELOW The Ferrari team celebrate Schumacher's 2000 Australian Grand Prix victory

# SUPERCARS

ABOVE The dominant Ferrari team celebrate after the 2004 Hungarian Grand Prix

OPPOSITE Michael Schumacher – the most prolific Grand Prix winner of all time

another constructors' championship. He'd won in Australia, Brazil and Imola, the European Grand Prix at the Nurburgring, in Canada, Italy, Japan, the USA and Malaysia – while Barichello added an emotional first win of his own in Germany. It was a totally dominant performance, and the start of five consecutive seasons of drivers' and

constructors' championship doubles for Schumacher and Ferrari.

In 2001 they won nine more races, and in 2002, with the F2002, another fourteen (out of a fifteen race calendar) – almost as dominant a season as you could have. In 2003, with the F2003, it wasn't quite so straightforward as Schumacher scored points in every race but 'only' won seven, with Barichello adding two more, while McLaren, Williams and Renault drivers also got onto the top step of the 2003 podium. But in 2004 it was virtually all Schuey again, as he added thirteen more Grands Prix wins to his personal tally, while Barichello again gave the team two more.

Such domination had long ago made Schumacher by far the most prolific Grand Prix winner of all time, and his sixth and seventh drivers' titles in 2003 and 2004 took the German past Juan Manuel Fangio's five-times champion record that had stood since the 1950s. What's more, it comprehensively restored and underlined Ferrari's long-term commitment to and dominance of Formula 1. By the end of 2004 (from 704 Grand Prix starts) they had 182 Grands Prix wins, 178 pole positions, 181 fastest laps, a dozen drivers' titles and thirteen constructors championships. No other team in Grand Prix history even comes close, and if Ferrari suffered an uncharacteristically uncompetitive start to a 2005 season where new regulations had thrown the whole pecking order into confusion, it was hard to find a serious observer who didn't know they'd soon bounce back.

# Chapter 14

# Production Cars

AND AS EVER, WHILE ALL THIS Grand Prix action was putting the gloss on the marque from Maranello, the production cars were providing the real reason for being there – and in the mid-1990s they were looking to extremes again. As the fiftieth anniversary of the company's origins approached, Ferrari had also created a successor for the limited-edition flagship line started by the 288GTO and its evolution the F40. Logically enough, they would call it the F50, and it would be another giant leap.

Amazing as it might sound, in some ways it was even more extreme than the F40, and Ferrari stated that its main purpose was to let the F50 owner come as close as possible to experiencing Formula 1 performance on the road. They would even be able to do that with the roof off, because the F50 could be run as a berlinetta, or with the removable solid roof panels taken out as a barchetta – surely the fastest open car in the world.

It was unveiled a couple of years before the actual anniversary, early in 1995, and Pininfarina had created a

shape that was dramatic and controversial – very different from the F40, with a wild combination of curves, cooling vents, high wings, and a vee-shaped bonnet line clearly intended to evoke the shape of a modern Formula 1 car. But whether you thought it was pretty or not, it was certainly aerodynamically efficient, with reasonably low drag and the all-important high-speed stability.

It backed up its race-related claims with a catalogue of Formula 1 related technology. The chassis used super-light composite construction with Kevlar, carbon fibre and Nomex, and the bodywork was mainly carbon fibre. The suspension used pushrods and rockers just like the latest grand prix cars, and solid suspension bushes, but with electronically variable damping to retain a least a

touch of ride comfort. And a bit like the F40, the F50 had little or nothing between driver and car to take away the control or dull the feel. There was no traction control, no four-wheel drive, no anti lock brakes, nothing that could detract from the purity.

What it did have was one of the greatest engines Ferrari had ever put into a road car. And it had a totally different philosophy from the small capacity turbocharged 288GTO and F40 – going instead for a large capacity but non turbo V12 to give more of the instant, linear response of the grand prix car rather than the much peakier delivery of the turbo engine, and it was genuinely related to Ferrari's Formula 1 engines of the late 1980s.

Of course, it couldn't nearly match the output per litre of the real thing, so they made it bigger than the race engines, with a capacity of 4.7 litres. It had four

very special camshafts, five valves per cylinder and very sophisticated electronics. And while it wouldn't approach the racing V12s' 18,000rpm-plus speeds (with spring rather than pneumatic valve operation) it did rev hard enough to give a very distinctive character.

It was mounted longitudinally and produced a massive 520bhp with an exhaust note like no other car on the road. To be honest, though, it didn't go for absolute performance (which at 202mph and 0-60mph in 3.7 seconds was no longer outer limits by 1995) but it concentrated hard on the raw sensations of driving. The cabin is Spartan, with thinly padded seats and lots of exposed composites, but even with the roof open the curvy windcreen and rollover hoops give a feeling of being cocooned and the gearshift is the classic Ferrari open metal gate. The engine has a button start, a reasonably docile low-speed character, and ferocious, screaming top end power delivery. The steering is razor sharp, the brakes awesomely powerful, and at speed the F50 feels alive. Which is exactly the race-bred personality Ferrari was aiming for in this amazing car.

But it wasn't only the limited edition

ultra-cars that were pushing Ferrari forwards. When the V8 line changed again in 1999 it was another new start – moving the smaller Ferraris away from mid-sized rivals like Porsche's 911, and helping justify Ferrari's considerably higher prices.

The car was the 360 Modena, styling was by Pininfarina (and another move on from the 355), and the object of the exercise was to outperform the 355 in every significant area from performance to refinement to drivability – a familiar trend over the last few generations as even Ferrari customers became steadily more demanding.

Following the inevitable route of safety and comfort, it was a bit bigger again, but with new techniques and materials it was slightly lighter. The chassis was all-new, with a light but immensely strong alloy spaceframe and

BELOW 360 Modena Spyder, 2000

# PRODUCTION CARS

a lot of aluminium in the suspension units, too, with faster-responding adaptive damping. Capacity for the five-valve V8 was up to 3.6 litres, and power to 400bhp – again the best power per litre of any production engine in the world. Top speed was 185mph and 0-60mph took 4.5 seconds, neither of which was much quicker than the 355, but the way the 360 delivered it's performance was entirely different.

The fact that for the first time ever a Ferrari had a traction control option was a plus rather than a minus for most customers – because it provided a safety net if you ever needed it but could be switched off if you didn't want it, and even when it was on it wasn't intrusive. So yet again, the general opinion was that this was another 'best ever' compact Ferrari, and for more people than ever before. But in typical Ferrari style, 'best ever' only meant until the next 'best ever' came along, and in the case of the more compact sports cars, that didn't take long.

In 2004, Ferrari moved the goalposts again, with the F430 – a logical enough progression from the 360, but also another giant leap. It had handsome new looks and as was becoming the norm, nods and winks towards the latest Formula 1 technology – not least in the automated manual gearshifts, which aren't exactly like the racing equivalent, of course, but do serve to underline the connections. It also claimed to be the first production road car to use carbon ceramic brakes as standard, which was another motor sport spin-off – and

**BELOW** F430 Spyder, 2005

ABOVE F430 Ferrari, 2004

those were one of the most impressive features in a hugely impressive car. That is reassuring when you have a 4.3-litre V8 behind your shoulders producing no less than 483bhp, which makes the F430 a very quick car indeed, with a top speed very close to 200mph and 0-60mph in about 3.5 seconds, which very few cars could match even in these supercar-rich times.

But there was even more to the F430 than that, in its exceptionally sophisticated electronic control systems, which provided a valuable safety net but without spoiling the driving experience, especially for the more accomplished driver. Even for a Ferrari, it was a very complete package, combining performance with drivability, and most importantly of all keeping its Ferrari soul. And if you wanted all that plus fresh air, it was only a matter of time before the spyder version followed.

At the other end of the size scale in 2004, Ferrari launched another all-new grand tourer that took them in a new direction – or back to an older one. The car was the 612 Scaglietti, a front-engined coupe successor to the discontinued 456, and it was the biggest car Ferrari had built in many years – in the tradition of some of the great long distance mile-eaters of earlier days, and in part reminiscent of the larger four-

BELOW 612 Scaglietti, 2004

ABOVE Enzo, 2002

seaters like the 400 and 500 'saloons'. The Scaglietti name was in honour of one of Ferrari's earlier coachbuilders but the styling (inevitably) was by Pininfarina, and it was very attractive indeed.

Quick, too. Power comes from a 5.7-litre V12 that delivers 533bhp and massive flexibility. Enough, even in a big car

with four reasonably sized seats to promise a 199mph maximum and 0-60mph in 4.2 seconds – but also in a high degree of luxury, because the 612 Scaglietti was aimed at a very demanding customer willing to pay a very high price.

But large and luxurious as it is, the Scaglietti is also a classic Ferrari in terms of sporty character, with thoroughbred handling characteristics that even in the 21st century strongly reflect Ferrari's racing heritage

And then, fittingly, there was the launch of one more outer-limits Ferrari to top everything so far. By 2002, Ferrari could beat even the mighty F50, as it revealed its fastest ever road car, the Enzo – named appropriately enough for the founder, and a car he would surely have been proud of. They announced it a day after clinching a fourth consecutive Formula 1 Constructor's Championship, and like the F50 it emphasised the race-car links. They described it as 'the ultimate modern day embodiment of the marque's passion for performance, technology and dramatic style. . . this new car, as the pinnacle of our technological achievement, should be dedicated to our founder, who always felt that racing cars should lay the foundations of road car designs. . .'

Its (Pininfarina) shape took the Formula 1 cues even further, with the distinctive 'single-seater' nose shape and F1-like wing shape, plus complex aerodynamics including under-body 'ground effects'. The chassis was made entirely from carbon fibre and aluminium honeycomb and weighed only 202kg bare. The doors opened upwards, the front aerodynamic flaps and big rear wing adjusted automatically. The steering wheel had a flat-top, Formula 1-style, with push-button controls and engine rev tell-tale lights – and behind it there were paddle shifts for the sequential manual gearbox. Each buyer would go to the factory for the seats and pedals to be fitted to their shape, like a handmade suit.

BELOW Enzo, 2002

Power came from a 6-litre V12 - 660bhp delivered through massive rear wheels; no four-wheel drive for Ferrari. There was variably-damped pushrod suspension again, assisted steering and carbon-ceramic disc brakes as standard – a 'world first' for a road car. The unique 19-inch wheels (13 inches wide on the rear!) had single bolt attachments and tyre pressure sensors. And in Ferrari's words, 'the Enzo is the world's first car with complete electronic integration of the control systems for engine, gearbox, suspension, anti-lock brakes, traction control and aerodynamics. The six sub-systems all interact with each other comparing relevant information to enhance the overall performance of the car. . .'

By any standards, it was outrageously fast and focussed. It promised a maximum speed of almost 220mph, 0-60mph in 3.5 seconds and 0-124mph in 9.5 seconds – acceleration figures (if not a top speed) which finally threatened the still legendary McLaren F1.

It was a very different car from the first 1.5-litre V12 125 of more than fifty years before, but it probably couldn't have been anything but a Ferrari. And through this whole history, that has been a constant theme.

**LEFT** Enzo, 2002

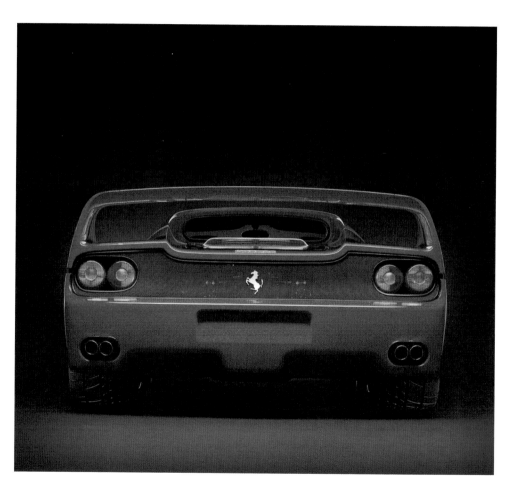

**The pictures in this book were provided courtesy of the following:**

GETTY IMAGES
101 Bayham Street, London NW1 0AG

CORBIS
111 Salusbury Road, London NW6 6RG

NATIONAL MOTOR MUSEUM
Beaulieu, Brockenhurst, Hampshire SO42 7ZN

With special thanks to:

© NEILL BRUCE
Grange Cottage, Harts Lane, Burghclear, Newbury RG20 9JN

GLEN SMALE
AUTOMOTIVE RESEARCH

Book design and artwork by Darren Roberts

Published by Green Umbrella

Series Editors Jules Gammond, Tim Exell, Vanessa Gardner

Written by Brian Laban